C ornia Maritime Academy Library (CSU)

D0021389

WITHDRAWN

MAKING MONEY WITH BOAT$

Fred Edwards

CORNELL MARITIME PRESS
Centreville, Maryland

Library of Congress Cataloging-in-Publication Data

Edwards, Fred.
Making money with boats/ Fred Edwards. — 1st ed.
p. cm.
Includes bibliographical references (p.) and index.
ISBN 0-87033-482-4
1. Boats and boating—Chartering—United States. I. Title.
HE596.E39 1996
387.5′42′068—dc20 96-9328

Manufactured in the United States of America
First edition

To those special kinds of magicians
who mix boats and water
to produce money

Contents

Preface

Since publication of my first book, *Charter Your Boat for Profit*, businesses of every industry have had to restructure, downsize, and resize in order to compete and survive. Today, as the introduction that follows discloses, the chartering industry continues to attract operators who know and love the water. More than ever before, however, charter operators must follow good business practices in order to transform water-related fun into the pure pleasure of profitability. Because business comes first, the first six chapters of this book are dedicated to the business side of chartering.

These six chapters contain information that every charter operator should know about starting a business, accounting and budgeting, how to prepare an insurance plan, marketing tools, how to write a marketing plan, and how to put it all together by writing a business plan.

Chapter 7, entitled "Computer Assistance," is a chapter that is vital for every charter operator. Today, a charter operator who conducts business without computer assistance is about as competitive as one who tells customers to scull the yachts they charter. The chapter was formulated to make readers snap their fingers and say, "I just know I can perform that function faster, more accurately, and cheaper by computer," and find a way to do it.

The final six chapters explain the laws and regulations that Congress, the Coast Guard, and the state boating law administrators have established for the charter industry. These include significant changes in requirements instituted for licensing, documentation, vessel inspection, crewed chartering, and bareboat chartering since the publication of *Charter Your Boat for Profit*. These chapters alone make this book a must-have for anybody seeking to make money with a boat. "Anybody" includes existing charter operators as well as newcomers who want to mix boating and business.

Here are answers to questions often asked about the Coast Guard and its regulations:

- *Where does the Coast Guard get the authority to regulate so much of the charter industry?* The Coast Guard, under the Department of Transportation, is charged with administering and enforcing laws and regulations for commercial vessels, their operators, and their crews.
- *What is a CFR?* The Coast Guard derives the bulk of its operating rules and regulations from the Code of Federal Regulations (CFR). Think of the CFR as coming from a computer that collects all the laws that Congress passes, sorts them into broad categories, and prints out each category as an operating manual. For example, CFR Title 46, *Shipping*, comprises nine volumes. The first seven volumes constitute Chapter I of Title 46, which is: Coast Guard, Department of Transportation. (In this book, terms such as *Title 46*, *CFR Title 46*, *46 CFR*, and *CFR 46* have the same meaning.)
- *Is there any rhyme or reason to the Coast Guard's regulations?* Although the Coast Guard's rules often appear to be disorganized, overlapping, and sometimes hopelessly bureaucratic, they can be subdivided into three functions. The Coast Guard refers to these functions as "trade, safety, and manning." In this book those functions roughly translate into requirements for documentation, vessel inspection, and captains' licenses, respectively.

The author's sincere thanks go to all those who provided input to this book. A special acknowledgment is in order for the following:

Mike Kimball, CPA, provided research copies of two books he coauthored that are important to every charter operator: *Tax Guide for the Business Use of Yachts*, and *Tax Guide for the Business Use of Yachts, Volume II: Charter Operations.*

Jeffrey C. Smith, Executive Director of the National Association of Charterboat Operators (NACO), edited a copy of the chapters on federal regulation of the industry. His assistance ensures that this book will be of special value to NACO's membership, which forms a core segment of the book's readership.

Gregory D. Szczurek, who wrote the industry's definitive book on licensing, *U.S. Coast Guard Licenses and Certificates,* edited the chapters on Coast Guard requirements and provided cogent suggestions that were incorporated into the book.

The United States Coast Guard, which has the thankless job of enforcing laws and regulations affecting the charter industry, has, for over fifteen years, provided the author with information, from officials at every level, and has always given positive, knowledgeable, and friendly responses to his queries. Of particular value for this edition were: Commander R. J. Fitzpatrick, Chief, Vessel Compliance Branch, USCG Headquarters (G-MCO-2); Lieutenant Dean Firing, Compliance Enforcement Branch, USCG Headquarters (MVI-1); Lieutenant Commander James C. Howe, Public Affairs Officer, Seventh Coast Guard District (dpa); and Lieutenant Junior Grade Chuck Diorio, Media Relations Branch, USCG Headquarters (G-CP-2).

Throughout the book the term "charter operator" is used to describe a person in business, as opposed to a customer who charters a boat from an owner, operator, or agent. Furthermore, the term includes operators who do not charter their boats to others, but who sell tickets, or boarding rights, to passengers for hire aboard head boats, party boats, and all the other money-making craft described in the introduction. In short, a charter operator in this book is a person dedicated to turning a buck with a boat.

The terms vessel, boat, and craft are used interchangeably in order to avoid monotony.

To write this book, the author drew from his experience as business executive, entrepreneur, Coast Guard licensing specialist, and licensed skipper of his own vessel. He converted his training and experience into a package that is the only one of its kind. This book is crammed with today's business principles and written for today's charter operators. Don't conduct a chartering business without it.

Don't even *think* about using boats for profit without reading this book. If you are thinking about starting a charter operation, read the book from cover to cover. If your business is already under way, research this book carefully to confirm what you know and learn things you don't. As long as there is a dollar on the table, a competitor for your market share, financial risk to manage, and an abstruse glob of Coast Guard regulations to obey, you'll need this book.

Libraries and bookstores offer hundreds of books about marketing and a few that deal with Coast Guard regulations, but none that will do what this book does. This book was written for *you*. The author understands your language and your way of life. He is a licensed 100-ton master with years of experience on the water. He has taught Coast Guard license exam prep classes. He is a writer who has specialized in Coast Guard matters for fifteen years. He has formed and operated four successful businesses, and he has served chief executive officers as a marketing and strategic planning specialist.

Best of success with your business!

MAKING MONEY
WITH BOAT$

INTRODUCTION

How People Make Money with Boats

Since publication of *Charter Your Boat for Profit* in 1989, the charter industry has absorbed a lot of hits. The bust of the offshore oil industry in the 1980s took its toll on marinas along the Gulf Coast. Adverse income tax laws, recession, user fees for licensing, drug-testing costs, hurricanes, the Gulf war, and a 70 percent plunge in large boat sales due to a misguided "luxury tax" all combined to assail the industry relentlessly.

Being familiar with these conditions, I had misgivings as to what my research for this book would reveal about the future of chartering, but my misgivings were proven groundless. It was a pleasurable surprise to contact so many charter operators who had weathered the hard times and were picking up speed like water-skiers up from a spill. I found that there is still something about water and boats that simply defies logic. A paragraph from *Charter Your Boat for Profit* hints at it:

> Psychologists speak of water as the cradle of life. They hypothesize that humans seek the water because of a subconscious urge to return to some prehistoric life form in warm seas, or a drive to return to prenatal comfort in amniotic fluids. Those of us who simply like the water don't need all that theory. We merely accept the water's magical attraction, and return again and again, just like a compass needle always returns to north—not because it knows magnetic theory, but simply because it has to.[1]

In spite of romanticism, all successful charter operators report that they approach their operation like a business and work it days, nights, holidays, and weekends. Most successful operators understand accounting and budgeting, insurance planning, marketing, and business planning. They know how to manage liabilities under maritime law, and they make sure they operate their charter businesses within the Coast Guard's regulations.

Most charter operators also proclaim that for success they need supplemental income. They might diversify simply by selling snacks and drinks at the site where their boats are docked. But whatever they do, they need to add another profit center (sometimes called *business unit*, or *strategic business unit*) to feed the bottom line.

Jeffrey C. Smith, executive director of the National Association of Charterboat Operators,[2] amplifies: "Very few people can do chartering full time, except for psychic income. Some add assistance towing, some run boatyards, and about 50 percent of our 4,100 members do fishing-related charters."

Charter operators also are quick to identify *leverage* as the ultimate method of increasing income. Without leverage, Joe Charterhouse, who has found the highest competitive prices and the lowest possible costs, who works twelve hours a day every day and earns ten dollars an hour, will gross $43,800 a year. That is the most he will *ever* make. He has run smack-dab into a time barrier. Sure, he might increase earnings by working longer hours, but with days limited to twenty-four hours apiece, eventually he will hit that time barrier again like a boat hitting a reef.

He might ask, "If I can make a profit with one boat, why can't I make more with two, and more yet with three?" In that way he can leverage by getting other people to use their time to make dollars for him. Everybody with an employee is leveraging. People who sell franchises are leveraging. Everybody who wants to beat the time barrier must leverage.

After reviewing the last five paragraphs, it seems appropriate to paraphrase Kipling by adding, "If you can do all of this, my friend, you'll be a success." The good news is that you *can* do all of this, as illustrated in the following examples.

AIRBOATS

Entrepreneurs use airboats to take tourists, hunters, and fishermen into swamps and over shallow grassy lakes. They mount a radial engine and propeller above the stern of a shallow-draft hull and have an airboat that flies across the water without exposing a marine propeller or transmission to loss.

Except for the engine, there is little maintenance, and out-of-water storage is simple, since there is no keel or propeller to protect. In fact, some one-boat operators trailer their airboats from site to site and leave them on the trailers when they are not in use. On the other hand, fleet operators might just leave the boats in their backyards between charters.

Most airboat operators I have seen use them to supplement income from a high-visibility profit center, such as a combination gasoline station and convenience store site.

BED AND BREAKFAST (B&B)

For years, people who like to meet people have been renting out spare rooms on a nightly basis and including breakfast in the package. If you stir in the magic of water, you have a B&B operation on your boat.

Bette and Clyde Rice got the idea in 1982 as a way to combine production of income with full-time boating.[3] They wanted to live in Friday Harbor, in the San Juan Islands of the Pacific Northwest. So they bought a 60-foot ketch-rigged motor sailor named *Jacquelyn* and converted two of the three staterooms for B&B guests. Their advice to others:

1. The people who select a floating B&B are several cuts above many patrons of a shoreside B&B.
2. Make a business plan first.

Jerry Brown didn't decided to convert to B&B until *after* he bought his boat, in 1985.[4] His 96-foot tugboat, *Challenger*, is berthed on Lake Union in downtown Seattle. He offers eight luxury cabins with accommodations ranging from private single bunks to the master's cabin. For supplemental income, he also advertises B&B accommodations on two "smaller" boats—a 46-foot Arden and a 46-foot Defever trawler. Guests on the latter two boats attend breakfast buffet aboard *Challenger*. His advice:

1. Used boats can be found for multicabin conversion at relatively low prices.
2. Position yourself with a theme boat (see chapter 5), but be careful about selecting a tugboat, because of restrictive cabin requirements.[5]
3. Count on working seven days a week.

BOAT HOUSES

A purist might claim that boat houses are not boats, but they float and they can generate income. I am not referring to roofed-over boat cover structures, nor to floating low-cost housing that has appeared from time to time in locations from Marin County, California, to Key West, Florida. Rather, I mean floating homes such as those situated in the yacht harbor at West End, in New Orleans. They sell for over a hundred thousand dollars each and rent for over a thousand a month.

A newer development of boat houses built on barge hulls is moored in Barefoot Cay Marina, 35 miles south of Miami. A customer can move into one of these houses at the marina, or tow it anywhere. In 1994, these boat houses were listed for sale from $29,500 to $125,000.[6]

Perhaps the truest hybrids are in the canebrakes fronting the Louisiana bayous. These are floating platforms carrying small recreational trailers on deck. With electricity provided by portable generators, they serve as weekend getaways, and fishing and hunting platforms.

BURIALS AT SEA

Several companies advertise regionally and nationally for this service, while individual skippers work for the companies or for themselves. Charter operator David Zalewski got his start eight years ago when a man approached him on the docks and asked if he would scatter his father's cremated remains at sea. Since then, Captain Dave—as he is known—figures that he has scattered fifteen thousand sets of ashes from his Bertram 28 Sportfish, *Lucky Too*.[7]

Although Zalewski performs services for individual clients and families, most of his business derives from a dozen funeral homes in the Tampa Bay area that hire him to conduct mass scatterings. He records the scatterings in his log and gives the funeral homes the coordinates of the locations.

Zalewski—a charter fishing skipper when not scattering—estimates that 20 percent of his business is scattering. His van advertises "Sport Fishing/Cremation Scattering." He has a federal permit and an occupational license, is commercially insured, and is a Coast Guard-licensed captain. He also holds a license to do cremations himself.

Although Zalewski legally scatters ashes as near as 3 miles from shore, he notes that burial of an uncremated body at sea must be done in federal waters at 100 fathoms or more.

CASINOS

Some floating casinos will never cast off a line while others may be authorized to follow river or lake courses while their customers are gambling. At last count, casino-vessels had been authorized by a half-dozen states from coast to coast, and more were being considered. This is big business. For example, by July 22, 1994, the four vessels operating in Missouri had taken in adjusted gross revenue of $15.3 million. Two of them had been in service only since June and the other two since May. And not one was using slot machines.[8]

Earlier arrivals in the casino business were the so-called "cruises to nowhere" (see chapter 8 for more on this topic). These vessels offer cruises from their stateside berths to federal waters, where customers can take in a few hours of gambling. Such day-cruise operations have increased in number and are profiting. For example, in 1995 the *St. Petersburg Times* reported that ten operators were running seventeen of these day-cruise ships from various ports in Florida alone. Revenues from cruises to nowhere show that this is also big business. The *Times* article reported that in 1994 Empress Cruise Lines, one of the companies, racked up eighteen million dollars in sales from its two vessels.[9]

Like other charter operations, boats taking cruises to nowhere also provide diversified products and services. By doing so, they not only increase income, but also keep gamblers from getting bored while en route to the gambling sites. Here's an example of offerings, taken from an Empress Cruise Line advertisement: "Free gourmet buffet. Area's largest casino. Live music. Karaoke. Party fun. Skeet shooting." On a cruise I took, the crew cleared away the skeet shooters long enough for the skipper to perform two formal marriages on the bow—at an appropriate cost to the wedding parties.

CHARTER BROKERS

A charter broker serves as go-between for charter companies and their clients. (See following section on charter companies and clubs.) A broker may handle a single product (such as does Nautor's Swan Charters),[10] or may work with dozens of companies. Somewhat like those of a travel agent, a broker's services generally are free to the client because the broker is paid by the charter company. If the broker subscribes to the industry's ethical standards, the client pays the same amount through the broker as by contacting the company directly.

Several professional charter broker organizations oversee ethical standards for charter brokers. Lynn Jachney of Lynn Jachney Charters, Inc.,[11] is president of one of these organizations—the American Yacht Charter Association (AYCA). She reports:

> AYCA's membership is invitational to American brokers who work internationally, who have been in business many years, and who have demonstrated ethical business behavior. AYCA, with some two dozen members, shares with the Mediterranean Yacht Brokers' Association. Any broker member who lowers a commission to offer a lower charter rate would be expelled.

If you should become a broker for one or more companies in the Caribbean, you might seek membership in the Charter Yacht Brokers' Association (CYBA). Jachney says that CYBA has been in existence for more than fifteen years. It has a large number of members, all of whom are required to have been in business for at least two years before acceptance. Like AYCA, CYBA's purpose is to increase standards and ethics. Many brokers belong to both organizations.

Jachney, who has been in business since 1968, brokers only crewed yachts (no bareboats). She says that most of her customers are referrals, although a large number are return customers for up to the fifteenth time. Such marketing success hinges upon the quality of the broker's service, and the quality of the bases, the boats, and the crews. Regarding crews, she says, "In the industry, we say that the right crew will sell a raft."

Although Jachney does not handle bareboats, many brokers do. Bob Tate[12] of Chicagoland Bareboaters Club, Ltd., a CYBA member, represents bareboats *and* crewed boats. He says, "Small companies need both bareboat and crewed boat income." But, he advises, "Bareboats bring less revenue because the commission is only on the boat."

Whether the operation involves bareboats, crewed boats, or both, successful charter brokers chorus that they must visit the company fleets periodically. And the cost comes out of their bottom lines. Chicagoland's Tate says, "You must be sure there is a manager on site, and you should visit the site annually if possible."

Mimi Stokes, manager of travel and the charter department of BOAT/U.S. Yacht Charters, [13] visits crews and bareboats annually. Queried as to whether she considers it a vacation to visit worldwide prime chartering spots, she replied that doing her job properly is work, not fun.

CHARTER COMPANIES AND CLUBS

Think of a charter company as a manager of a fleet or several fleets of yachts. The company might own all of the vessels, or it might accept other owners' boats for charter. It also might sell boats and manage them for the owners under a purchase program. Or it might operate as a club, whose members provide boats for other members at discounted rates. In all three situations, the fleet offers a chance for supplemental income from instructing. Entrepreneurs participate in all aspects of these ventures—as boat owners, sellers, buyers, managers, sailing instructors, seamanship instructors, and operators.

Turning Over Your Boat to a Charter Company

Although some large charter companies use only boats sold through them (see following section on purchase programs), many smaller companies are always looking for boats to add to their fleets.

Turning over your boat to a full-service charter company is like converting it to a time-share condominium. The manager advertises the entire condominium, maintains the complex, and rents out the rooms. The manager charges each owner for a share of the maintenance (unless the owner does it) and returns a percentage of the rent collected to the owner.

Charter company contracts vary, depending upon the boat owner's wishes and the firm selected. You might place your boat as a bareboat or a crewed boat (see chapter 9). If it is crewed, you could serve as captain, or the company might provide a captain. You might keep the boat at your dock, or the organization might provide a dock. In short, by finding the right company, you can place your boat out for charter in a way that will fit your exact needs.

How do you find the right company? For the major chartering regions, consider the firm's number of years of operation, whether it is a member of an established chartering association, and its reputation with boat owners and charterers. If it is a new company, check the owner's professional record, visit its fleet, and contact several charter agents who know the industry. To choose a local company, take the following steps:

1. Find established companies in the Yellow Pages.
2. Select a company capable of handling your type of boat.
3. Query the company's boat owners and customers.
4. Execute a contract that suits you and the company.

Yacht Purchase Programs

Before the Tax Reform Act of 1986, yacht purchase programs were widely used as tax loopholes. Since elimination of the loopholes by the 1986 act, purchase programs have evolved into viable options for investors who want to:

1. Buy a yacht.
2. Use it (or a comparable one at a different site) several weeks a year.
3. Have someone else pay for part of it.

Most purchase program contracts run for four or five years. A specific program may vary from a completely shared-risk venture, on the one hand, to a fully guaranteed plan, on the other. Under a completely shared-risk program, the purchaser might make a down payment and agree to make mortgage payments, while sharing operating costs along with the resulting net chartering income, if there is any. Under a partial guarantee program, the company might provide the purchaser a down payment on the front end, with a guarantee of no operating costs during the charter period.

In another example, if the purchaser makes a large enough down payment, the company might guarantee no operating costs *and* no mortgage payments. Depending upon the program, the purchaser will either own the boat outright at the end of the period or pay the balance owed. The program also might contain an option for the boat to be sold at the end of the period.

Diane C. Milners, director of sales for CYOA in St. Thomas, Virgin Islands,[14] explains:

> There are two types of programs in the Caribbean, those with guarantees and those without. You must know your risk level, and your comfort level with risk, just like when you are investing in mutual funds or stocks, because (with a boat) you are selecting part of your investment portfolio.

Milners, a licensed 100-ton master, adds that a yacht purchase program is still the kind of business where you can buy a boat for considerably less than buying one on your own. She cautions, however, that in addition to the investment factor, you must consider the fun factor, and should love sailing and going on the water.

Others in the charter industry also emphasize the fun factor. For example, charter broker Lynn Jachney says: "Don't buy a boat unless you enjoy owning it. Don't do it just to make money; do it if you can afford it." Broker Bob Tate further advises prospective owners to plan to use their boats during the times allotted by the agreement and not to count on increasing revenue by selling those times.

Furthermore, fleet operators recommend that owners plan to use their boats during the less desirable times, keeping them available for prime-time chartering. However, Jachney speaks of some owners who love sailing so much that they will sacrifice revenue *any time* they get a chance to get away from their shore-bound lives.

Above all, a person thinking of participating in a yacht purchase program should bring an accountant into the picture at the beginning. CPA Mike Kimball, coauthor of two books on the business use of yachts, says, "If I were fixing to spend $150,000-plus on a charter boat, I would want to know the tax implications."

Kimball, who uses his Bayliner 30 for business entertainment on 30,000-acre Palestine Lake in East Texas, adds:

> Tax rules that apply to boats are intricate and restrictive, because of IRS rules designed to limit past excesses. I found that a lot of people were either not aware of the rules, or misinterpreted them. Their accountants didn't have enough clients to be that familiar with this area, so we looked at tax court cases and published the supplement.

The supplement he refers to is *Tax Guide for the Business Use of Yachts, Volume II: Charter Operations,* and is available from Tax Savvy Publications, Ltd.[15]

Charter Clubs

Under the club concept, a qualified member may use another club member's boat at less cost than by renting from a traditional charter company. In the meantime, the boat's owner will earn more cash than if he or she had kept the vessel out of charter. As middleman, the club derives revenue from initiation fees, dues, and perhaps a percentage of the charter fees. The club may keep its operation streamlined and relatively cost-free if it neither docks nor maintains the fleet.

The member's financial outlays provide an incentive to use the club-provided boats. The club can nurture this reaction by organizing group events and publishing a newsletter.

A variation of this concept is offered by Tom Christensen, owner of WhyCharter Boat Exchange, Ltd.[16] His company compiles a list of boats for exchange, similar to the way that firms offer homes for exchange. He charges a small fee to list a boat in the company's directory, which is published semiannually. The listing offers space to describe the boat and the local cruising grounds, as well as the owner's preferred exchange locations. Members interested in exchanging their boats make their arrangements directly with each other.

DIVE BOATS

Operating a dive boat is as specialized as scuba diving itself. Dive-boat skippers and dive-shop operators overwhelmingly declare that the captain should be a certified diver, and preferably an advanced diver. As a diver affiliated with one of the certification agencies (see below), the skipper can fill and inspect air tanks and check their levels before repetitive dives. The skipper also can be alert to avert decompression sickness ("the bends"). And if there is another licensed captain aboard, the skipper might dive with the passengers as dive master or instructor.

Diving is a self-regulated industry, whereby certification agencies train divers in the classroom and under water to increasing levels of competence. A diver can't even have a tank filled at an authorized station before earning a basic certification card (C-Card) from a recognized agency.

Each agency offers its own program that leads to a progression of diving certification levels. The following agencies or their representatives can be found listed in advertisements in diving magazines and in the Yellow Pages: National Association of Scuba Diving Schools (NASDS), National Association of Underwater Instructors (NAUI), National YMCA Center for Underwater Activities, Professional Association of Diving Instructors (PADI), and Scuba Schools International, Inc. (SSI).

A dive-boat skipper who affiliates with a recognized agency gains the dive-business equivalent of having joined a chamber of commerce and a better business bureau. And the agency provides a license to teach the skill; sell, service, and rent the equipment; and operate as travel agent and tour guide to take customers to dive sights all over the world.

Of course, if you are planning to exploit such a potential customer base successfully, you must exercise basic business practices. Mike McCrory, a dive-shop owner in Little Rock, Arkansas, who has been in the business since 1980, counts off on his fingers the number of profit centers it takes for success:

> To run a dive shop, you must have retail sales, and your corporate burden has to be reflected in retail prices. You must have a great service department. You have to provide travel, so you need a travel department as a profit center. You also need a good education department, and a rental department.[17]

McCrory, who wears a second hat as educational director of NASDS, uses two boats for local lake dives. When he sponsors dive trips away from home, the destination dive shops provide the boats.

EXCURSION BOATS

People will pay to go afloat to eat and drink and dance and gamble. Customers go to watch whales, observe rocket launches, eyeball sunsets, and see sailboat races. They climb aboard paddle-wheel boats to take harbor cruises, bay cruises, river cruises, and lake cruises. And they embark on glass-bottomed boats and passenger submarines to gaze at fish, coral, and scuba divers.

Operators who sell products and services on board an excursion boat have a captive market for subsidiary sales. For example, during a five-hour Cajun-country cruise on the Mississippi River, how many customers would refuse a helping of gumbo or red beans and rice, along with a cold drink to tone down the hot spices?

FERRYBOATS

The ancient Greeks believed that the first ferry operator was Charon, who carried the dead across the river Styx to Hades. Charon would accept a passenger only if he or she had the fare—a silver coin placed in the mouth before burial. Perhaps Charon was the first charter boat skipper.

Today, ferryboats come in all configurations: from rowboats to vehicle transporters with propellers at both ends; from train-carrying vessels that have transited the English channel to high-speed catamarans and state-of-the-art hydrofoils. Customers range from Chinese pedestrians traveling between Hong Kong and Kowloon to automobile owners traveling between Nova Scotia and Newfoundland, to camel herders taking their beasts across the Senegal River in Africa.

Charter Your Boat for Profit reported on the Catalina Channel Express as an example of a successful entrepreneurial American ferry service. This charter operation commenced in 1981, with a fifty-five-passenger boat serving islanders commuting to the mainland. It expanded into a fleet of four fast ferryboats carrying tourists between San Pedro, California, and Catalina Island.

The company's latest upgrade, reported in the November/December (1994) edition of *WorkBoat Magazine*, consists of two $2.5 million vessels that combine a cruising speed of 32 knots with a computer-controlled system for eliminating roll and dampening pitch and yaw. Explaining the computerization, President Doug Bombard of Catalina Express said, "By 1990, we realized speed was only half the problem. The other was passenger comfort. It doesn't matter how fast you get folks to the island if they're sick when they arrive."[18]

This is another example of offering the customer what he or she wants or needs (see chapter 4).

FISHING GUIDES

One serene summer evening I anchored my sailboat fore and aft alongside the north bank of the Caloosahatchee Canal, west of Lake Okeechobee in Florida. The night was hushed for hours, until I and the small alligator dozing in the water near my bow were awakened by the roar of a speeding powerboat. The boat carried a bass guide who was taking a business executive out at dawn for an hour of fishing before returning him to the rat race.

Fishermen who know how to catch fish report that working as fishing guides helps pay their bills, while keeping their local knowledge well honed. When not engaged with a client, they can fish for fun, compete in tournaments, or earn supplementary income. For example, I talked with a guide at Okeechobee whose wife ran the family boat-and-tackle store while he was on the lake. When he was back in the store, it became a gathering place for other guides, because he was the unofficial chairman of the local guide group. On top of this, he won a good many tournaments.

What qualifications do guides need? Because most guides depend heavily upon word-of-mouth advertising, they simply have to please their customers. They do this through a professional attitude and by developing rapport; providing the boat, tackle, and bait; and, above all, bringing their customers back with fish.

HEAD BOATS AND PARTY BOATS

A head boat charges per person to take scheduled fishing trips, while a party boat generally contracts for a group. The same boat may be used for both purposes. Charter operators for these boats normally provide fishing gear and bait, and often will bait the hooks—as well as clean and cook the fish.

As with gambling boats, schedules have to be kept. But, unlike gambling boats, local knowledge and electronic fish-finder gear are often necessary to meet the schedules. If you offer a charter from eight o'clock to noon, and another from one o'clock to five, you must get the first party back—with fish—in time to embark the second party on time.

HOUSEBOATS

A pristine lake or a winding river can provide an excellent opportunity for an entrepreneur to become a houseboat charterer. A 40-foot-by-14-foot houseboat on calm waters offers a relaxing, pleasurable week to many families who would never consider trying a sailboat or a trawler. Houseboats are floating cottages, with something for everybody: fishing, snorkeling or scuba diving from the stern, sunbathing on the top deck, relaxing in the lounge, and exploring the water wilderness—with range, refrigerator, dishes, and linens aboard.

Bill Miller of Miller's Marina, Campgrounds, and Suwannee Houseboats, in Suwannee, Florida, explains the focus of his operation: [19]

> Our boats provide access to a river in the natural state. It's not commercialized, and there has been no development along the Suwannee since *Charter Your Boat for Profit* was published. To help keep the river natural, the state has set aside seventy-five million dollars to buy up sensitive property along the waterfront.

Miller adds, "Today, marinas must diversify and have more than one source of income." (The company name shows that he has positioned himself three ways.) "Since a storm in 1993 wiped out more than half of our boat stalls, we have been upgrading, and we expect to have a much nicer facility than we ever had, both the waterfront and the campground."

MOM-AND-POP CHARTER OPERATIONS

If small business is the backbone of America, the mom-and-pop charter is the keelson of chartering. Depending upon your customer profile (see chapter 5), you can embark a party in swimsuits or dinner dress, fishing clothes or business suits. Many mom-and-pops live aboard and leverage their chartering income with detailing work, bottom jobs, canvas work, and the like.

A one-boat charter operator might live ashore and simply use chartering revenue to offset some of the boating costs. It might be possible to strike a deal with a marina operator to dock the boat free. And the charter operator might position the business in one of a variety of different ways (see chapter 5), such as a pirate ship, a Chinese junk, a sunset cruise vessel, a shelling platform, a musical stage, or simply a sailing vessel.

PARASAIL

The following is an example of a parasail operator who positions himself in his market, exploits means of supplemental income, and employs leverage.

Captain Mike Bomar[20] owns two catamaran platforms 36 feet long by 25 feet wide, each of which is Coast Guard-certified for thirty-eight passengers (see chapter 10). He and another licensed captain operate the boats as launch and recovery platforms for parasail customers. A summary of his three-and-a-half-inch by eight-and-a-half-inch heavy-stock insert includes:

> Parasail, water skiing, boat rides, dolphin watch, shelling and snorkel trips, party cruises. Only U.S. Coast Guard-inspected parasail operation in Florida. Over 60,000 people in sixteen years of operation. You are in the hands of experience when you fly with us. We are the pioneers and developers of this motorized parasail catamaran and landing system.

RECREATIONAL BOATS

A major dynamic product added to the recreational boat inventory since the late 1980s is the jet-powered, personal watercraft (PWC). PWCs are everywhere, circling like gigantic water bugs, jumping wakes, and racing each other. They have perplexed lawmakers and the marine patrols alike, while their owners have been quietly collecting forty and fifty dollars an hour for their use. With an estimated six hundred thousand on the water by the end of 1994, they are a prolific form of primary income for small business entrepreneurs and supplementary revenue for marinas, surf shops, waterside motels, and other waterfront businesses.

A close cousin of the PWC, both in use and profitability, is the sailboard, which is essentially a surfboard with a sail. Not long ago, I was anchored at the Dry Tortugas—some 70 miles offshore from Key West—and watched a sixty-seven-year-old sailing into the anchorage on his sailboard! He had rented it for two weeks in Key West.

Also included with recreational boats are all the other craft that people rent when they visit the waterfront: Hobie Cats, iceboats, canoes, rafts, paddleboats, and even inner tubes. Each has a place in the charter business, because when people get near water, they want to get on it and in it.

RESTAURANTS AND FAST FOOD

The five-star cruising restaurant *U.S. Bon Appetit* is co-owned by Austrian restaurateur Peter Kreuziger. The vessel is a 67-ton steel trawler, powered by a Detroit 871 diesel. Although it can embark up to forty-seven diners from its landing in Dunedin, Florida, it often gets under way with only an intimate table for two, a chef, stewards, and a violinist. Captain K, as he is called, charges by the hour, with a three-hour minimum for larger parties. Costs for smaller parties are discreetly negotiable. The vessel supplements its income from an inn and a continental-class restaurant adjacent to its docks.

I once sailed up the Tchefuncta River to Marina del Ray (yes, they spell it "Ray") in Madisonville, Louisiana, and was assigned berthing inside the marina alongside an abandoned barge. That evening, I found that the "abandoned" barge had been rented as a party platform complete with catered cuisine and live music. The occasion that night was a five-hundred-person wedding reception, hosted as only a Cajun family can host one.

And what about fast food? On Saturday afternoons in July and August, as many as a thousand expensive powerboats raft up at a place called "Party Cove" in the Lake of the Ozarks. Entrepreneurs like Shelly Seiler, from Columbia, Missouri, and Grant Bunting, from New Zealand, circulate in pontoon barges selling T-shirts and soft drinks.[21] They are not strictly chartering out their boats, but entrepreneurial success like this deserves mention in a book about making money with boats.

SAILING INSTRUCTION

Instructing is an ego-rewarding way to help defray boating expenses. Thousands of skippers use their boats to teach day sailing and cruising. A skipper-owner can tailor the instruction to each student's level of knowledge and abilities and can arrange the schedule to fit that of the student.

To increase income leverage, many schools that started from a single boat have expanded into a fleet, or even flotillas of different classes of boats. Programs offered include day sailing, offshore cruises, and ocean passages. Some schools offer their own certification of the graduate's qualifications as a charterer, or a guarantee of a free course if a graduate is refused a charter. Other schools associate with external certification programs such as those offered by the American Sailing Association and US SAILING.[22] Many schools also bring in supplemental income by chartering boats.

SALTWATER SPORTFISHING

Sportfishing charter operators say that this is the only way to go. It may be for billfish, mackerel, tarpon, or any of the other fighting fish. The water may be turquoise or indigo, and the sky may be robin's-egg blue or steel-gray. But the offshore thrill of the fight is always the same to the customer and the skipper. A charter operator in this arena may serve as fishing guide, confidant, weather and seamanship expert, engineering specialist, tournament facilitator, sandwich maker, and even taxidermy advisor.

TELEVISION AND FILMS

Charter Your Boat for Profit described a 24-foot Wellcraft Airslot that Ralph T. Heath Jr., director of the Suncoast Seabird Sanctuary, Inc., in Indian Shores, Florida, had configured for inshore photography. Eight years later, Heath reports a classic example of two marketing strategies discussed over and over in this book.

First, he expanded operations by *diversifying*. He purchased a 70-foot, 100-ton fiberglass trawler-yacht and rigged it for offshore cinematography. As part of the refit of the vessel, *Whisker*, he modified the decks with heavy nonskid material, facilitating the use of camera tripods on three levels. He also installed compressors to fill dive tanks at sea and a water maker for fresh-water washdowns. In a rare match of numbers, he holds a 100-ton master's license to operate his 100-ton boat.

Second, he upgraded the electronics aboard the 24-foot Wellcraft for use in periods of low visibility and installed a second tower for fore-and-aft-mounted cinematographic platforms. With these two vessels, he *positioned* himself as a specialist both offshore and inshore. Moreover, he often combines camera sessions with his internationally known Seabird Sanctuary. Heath simply says, "We specialize in all types of marine photography, above water and under water."

Is Heath succeeding? Absolutely. Here are examples. He had just finished a half-hour shoot with a CBS team from Alabama when he provided this most recent interview. He has hosted Jack Hanna, the curator of the Columbus Zoo in Ohio, who is known for a series titled "Animal Adventures." He recently did a session for *Sports Illustrated* and last fall carried out sessions twice with teams from the United Kingdom's BBC. He says, "We do this virtually on a daily basis."

Heath warns, however, that such customer interest doesn't happen overnight, and that a charter operator shouldn't attempt to go into business solely for television filming. He said, "Don't set up your boat for a camera crew and wait for someone to call on the telephone, unless you're extremely well known."

SUMMARY

1. Most successful charter operators diversify for supplemental income.
2. Although you can work only so many hours per day, you can escape this time barrier by leveraging other people's time into your charter operation.
3. To achieve success, a chartering business must be run as exactingly as any other business.
4. You can become a charter broker no matter where you live, but you must be prepared to travel at your own expense.
5. A charter company might charter boats, sell boats, and teach sailing.
6. Any charter operation can increase the bottom line if it is positioned uniquely within the marketplace.

CHAPTER 1

Starting Your Business

Historically, more than 50 percent of all small businesses fail during the first year, and 75 to 80 percent fail in the first five years. History also shows that some boats don't survive storms at sea, but anybody who has been through a storm knows that many boats endure. Applying that to business statistics, we see that, while 80 percent of small businesses fail, 20 percent are still in business after five years.

Each of us wants to be in that 20 percent, whether we are hoping just to help pay boat expenses or are shooting for a fleet of mega-yachts. So how can we crank the odds up in our favor?

I asked Peter Olsen, a Service Corps of Retired Executives (SCORE) counselor.[1] His eyes flashed like a bos'n's mate with a damage control problem, and he said, "I have two precepts. One, don't let yourself want to go into your business so badly that you'll let your emotions crowd out reason. And, two, back off and start planning."

This chapter is where the planning starts. Think of the chapter as a predeparture checklist and chapters two through five as underway checklists. They don't have to be read in numerical order, but the more you know about their contents, the better will be your business plan, which is covered in chapter 6.

Think of your business plan as the complete float plan or navigational plan. This first chapter can help you analyze your aptitude to run a chartering operation, determine the niche the business will fill (or should be filling), and complete your predeparture checklist.[2] The information you develop in these three steps will tell you who you are and what your business should be, and will provide a base to build upon when preparing or revising your marketing plan and your business plan.

APTITUDE

The armed forces operate on the premise that leadership can be taught. Similarly, the *skills* needed for a successful charter operation can be learned. However, a person with the *aptitude* for operating a business will always have a leg up on a person who does not. The more "yes" responses you can make to the following questions, the more comfortable you are likely to be as a charter operator.

- Are you a leader?
- Do you like other people?
- Do you enjoy competition?
- Are you a self-starter?
- Are you an organizer?
- Do you exercise willpower and self-discipline?
- Do you plan ahead?
- Do you assume responsibility for your actions?
- Do you like to make your own decisions?
- Do you have confidence in your decisions?
- When you make a decision, do you stick with it, and let nothing stop you?
- Are you willing to change a decision if the situation changes?
- Do others turn to you for help in making decisions?
- Is your health such that you never feel run down?

YOUR BUSINESS NICHE

Today, successful marketing depends upon finding out what the customers want and giving it to them in a way that no competitor can beat or equal. The difference between another ho-hum mom-and-pop sloop-for-charter down the pier and the only full-dressed pirate ship at the docks is the difference between an empty till and a chest of gold. The following six steps form the essence of a graduate course in marketing.[3]

1. Identify and describe your business.
2. Identify your service and products.
3. Identify your customers and their needs or desires.
4. Identify the competition and how it is filling the customers' needs or desires.
5. Determine how to make your service and products different or better than those of the competition.
6. Prepare a promotional program that will show the customers the unique benefits of using your services and products.

(See summary at the end of the chapter for a final predeparture checklist. The final checklist contains several additional items that will be covered in succeeding chapters.)

YOUR BUSINESS FIRST MATES

The purpose of the business chapters in this book is to stockpile a working knowledge of running a chartering business. The operative words here are "a working knowledge." A charter operator with a working knowledge of business skills should rely upon three experts for assistance with the details. Treat these experts as your business first mates. They are your accountant, your attorney, and your lender. Here's a way to get one of each at no charge.

Start by calling the nearest Service Corps of Retired Executives (SCORE) chapter. SCORE is a nationwide group of more than thirteen thousand volunteers in seven hundred installations who volunteer their time to assist people with small businesses. SCORE is an unusual governmental organization because it operates without subsidies and charges the consumer (us) no more than its costs.

Alternatively, if you decide to hire an accountant or an attorney, shop around by word of mouth, just like you do when you're buying a new boat. All other choices being equal, you might find an accountant or attorney who offers the first hour free. That will give you a good test, because if you can't prepare and state your case clearly in an hour, as sure as the tide rises and falls you don't have a handle on how you're going to run the business.

If the person you select *does* charge for the first session, but is reputable, you are not likely to get claim-jumped while you're prospecting. That lawyer will earn bigger fees after you've found the mother lode and need more involved assistance—and can afford to pay more. Lawyers—like you—are in business and should know the basic precept of customer loyalty: "Let your customer leave smiling, and he'll come back." Here's the bottom line: If you carefully develop a business plan with an accountant and an attorney, and stick with the plan, your return visits will be few and short.[4]

After developing your business plan, take it to a marine lender or a commercial loan officer—perhaps a vice president—at the bank. This is the chance to say, "I'm not asking for a loan but would like you to know what I'm going to do. Here's my plan. What do you think?" That ought to bring your final first mate on board—to be receptive when you *do* need a loan (see chapter 6).

YOUR BUSINESS ENTITY

Evaluate your planned business with your accountant and attorney to determine the best entity for your charter operation. Reevaluate as the operation grows, and as the tax laws change. Here are basic descriptions.

Sole Proprietor

This is the simplest business structure to set up and operate. The only requirements are that the charter operator be self-employed and the sole owner, and that the business not be incorporated. Except for obtaining a fictitious name (if the business will not be in the proprietor's name; more on fictitious names later), a sole proprietor simply obtains the necessary licenses (to be discussed) and sets up shop.

The major advantage of a sole proprietorship is full control over the running of the business. A major disadvantage is that the sole proprietor is personally liable for debts incurred by the proprietorship. Thus, a sole proprietor's personal assets can be taken to pay business debts. Other disadvantages are that the proprietor must provide all contributions of capital, labor, and skill, and that the proprietorship has limited life.

A charter operator who is a sole proprietor may be eligible to participate in a Keogh (HR-10) plan or an Individual Retirement Account (IRA).

At federal income tax time a sole proprietor fills out a Schedule C showing income and expenses and posts the profit (or loss) to Form 1040.

Partnership

Two or more individuals can join together in a partnership. By so doing, they reap the advantage of pooling capital, skills, labor, or all three. A partnership is a flexible form of business and has few legal formalities for its maintenance. It avoids double taxation because net profits go to the partners in agreed-upon proportions.

A partnership has the following disadvantages:

1. Partners have unlimited personal liability for business losses.
2. The partnership is legally responsible for the business acts of each partner.
3. A general partnership interest may not be sold or transferred without consent of all partners.
4. The partnership dissolves upon the death of a general partner.

The partnership agreement can be written or verbal. In fact, the IRS says:

> A partnership is the relationship between two or more persons who join together to carry on a trade or business. Each person contributes money, property, labor, or skill, and each expects to share in the profits and losses.[5]

The IRS includes a husband and wife in the preceding definition of a partnership and adds: "If spouses carry on a business together and share in the profits and losses, they may be partners whether or not they have a formal partnership agreement." [6]

However, the IRS says that family members will be recognized as partners only if one of the following requirements is met:[7]

1. If capital is a material income-producing factor, they acquired their capital interest in a bona fide transaction (even if by gift or purchase from another family member), actually own the partnership interest, and actually control the interest. A capital interest in a partnership is an interest in its assets that is distributable to the owner of the interest if he or she withdraws from the partnership, or if the partnership liquidates. The mere right to share in the earnings and profits is not a capital interest;
2. If capital is not a material income-producing factor, they must have joined together in good faith to conduct a business. In addition, they must have agreed that contributions of each entitle them to a share in the profits. Some capital or service must be provided by each partner.

The IRS will *not* accept a joint undertaking merely to share expenses as a partnership.

A Written Agreement

Although a written partnership agreement is not required, generally it is advisable in order to confirm major issues that might be forgotten or misunderstood later. The following issues should be addressed:

- The amount of time and/or money the partners will contribute.
- The methods of making business decisions.
- The method of sharing profits and losses.
- A distribution schedule or plan (payments of income to the partners).
- Contingency plans for when a partner dies, becomes disabled, or stops working or contributing to the business.
- The life span of the partnership.

Normally, a working member's share of the partnership income will be taxable for social security purposes. And the member may be eligible to participate in a Keogh plan or an IRA.

A partnership prepares IRS Form 1065 for information and sends it to the IRS. Using Form 1065, the partners would prepare a Schedule K-1, showing the share of profits and losses for each partner. Each partner then transfers the amounts from the Schedule K-1 to appropriate lines of the income tax return and keeps the Schedule K-1 for information.

Corporation

A corporation is an artificial person, created by a state government, to engage in business. Its advantages include:

- Limited liability for shareholders.
- Ability to raise capital more easily (by sales of stock and other securities) than with a partnership or sole proprietorship.
- Ease of ownership transfer by transfers of stock.

Disadvantages include:

- Higher costs than other business entities to create and maintain.
- Need for separate tax returns.
- Possibility of double taxation.

To form a corporation, the incorporators submit an application to the proper state official, usually the secretary of state. The application may be called a charter, or certificate of incorporation, depending upon the state. The charter contains the names and addresses of the incorporators, their citizenship status, the purpose for incorporating, the group's capital and business address, and names and addresses of the directors. When the state accepts the charter, the corporation is "born."

Ownership in a corporation is documented by capital stock certificates. The IRS states that, "Forming a corporation involves a transfer of money, property, or both by the prospective shareholders in exchange for capital stock in the corporation."[8]

The IRS does not allow incorporation for tax purposes. It does, however, allow it for general business purposes or to institute limited liability, for example. A charter operator should remember this if asked during an audit, "Why did you incorporate?"

Corporations file federal tax returns on either Form 1120 or Form 1120-A (short form).

Who Runs the Corporation?

The shareholders have ultimate control. They periodically elect a group of individuals to act as a board of directors and to make major decisions. The day-to-day decisions are made by corporate officers. If you, or you and your spouse, wear all of these hats, operating the business is simple. However, the corporate veil must be kept intact, i.e., you must carry out each of these functions to keep your artificial person "alive," including keeping minutes and other documents up to date.[9]

How a Charter Operator's Corporation Can Avoid Double Taxation

Jeffrey C. Smith, executive director of the National Association of Charterboat Operators, writes that "your corporation has to pay taxes only on the assets you have left in the bank at the end of the year—your 'profit.'"[10] He explains that an accepted way to avoid or lessen the corporate tax is to pay yourself a salary and bonus, thereby reducing or eliminating the "profit." Smith adds that the IRS will question it if you pay yourself an excessive salary (by the standards of the industry). He concludes, "But that is a problem most charter captains won't be lucky enough to worry about."

S Corporation

An S corporation offers the same limited liability as a corporation. However, it passes profits and losses through to the shareholders much like a partnership does for partners, thus avoiding double taxation. (The "S" is for "small" business, although a small business can incorporate either as a corporation or an S corporation.)

An S corporation is subject to more governmental regulation than a corporation. An S corporation cannot provide medical reimbursement for employees. And the only corporate retirement plan allowed is the Keogh plan. There is also a limitation on passive corporate income. However, for many small businessmen, the advantages of an S corporation far outweigh the disadvantages.

For federal tax returns, an S corporation files Form 1120S and provides an individual copy of Schedule K-1 to each shareholder, in the same manner that a partnership does for each partner.

You can elect S status for your charter company if it meets the following requirements:

- It has no more than thirty-five shareholders.
- It has only one class of stock.
- All of the shareholders are U.S. residents.
- All of the shareholders are individuals (people, rather than artificial entities).
- It operates on a calendar year financial basis.

YOUR BUSINESS NAME

Think ahead. "Jones & Son" might be about as appropriate as a wooden ship's figurehead on a fiberglass dinghy if Jones's son decides to join the navy and his daughter stays home to help run the business. Similarly, "Jones Charters" might become meaningless if Jones and spouse convert to a yacht sales business. "Jones Charters and Brokerage" might cause confusion at least, and legal heartburn at worst, if "Jane's Charters and Brokerage" happens to be an old-line operation down the wharf.

You can legally change business names relatively easily, and a change might entail nothing more than new stationery and checks. But it could also mean a new address or an amendment to a partnership agreement or a corporate charter (see following section). Moreover, a name change certainly can confuse and alienate customers. So it's important to choose a name that you are likely to keep for many seasons.

Fictitious Name

If you decide to incorporate, your business name will be filed with the corporate papers. However, if you operate as a sole proprietorship, and your business will use any name other than your own, you must file a fictitious-name statement. If you form a partnership, and not all the partners' names are used, or if none of the partners' names is used, you will have to file a fictitious-name statement.

To obtain approval for a fictitious name, you normally pay a small fee, have your proposed name checked for possible duplication, and advertise your intention to "do business as" (dba), for example, "Jones Yachting Services." Save money by advertising in a weekly neighborhood paper instead of the city paper. In many communities, small papers print fictitious-name notices for a substantial part of their advertising income and can handle the details quickly over the telephone.

YOUR BUSINESS LOCATION

Do you plan to conduct business from a boat? A dockside office? Your home? Will you use a post office box for a mailing address? What location will attract customers, is within your business plan budget, and falls within the zoning and licensing regulations?

If you will operate from an office or a building, here are some questions to consider: [11]

- Have you thought of renting or leasing with an option to buy?
- Can you modify the building for your needs at a reasonable cost?

- Is the location convenient to your customers?
- Is parking available?
- Has your attorney checked the lease and zoning?
- Will there be adequate fire and police protection?
- Do you have an adequate insurance plan? (See chapter 3.)
- How near to competitors is the location? If near, how will that affect sales?

If you will operate from your home, consider the following additional points:

- Be sure to comply with your city's zoning regulations and to obtain necessary licenses and permits (see later section on regulations, licenses, zoning, permits, and taxes).
- Most states outlaw the home production of fireworks, drugs, poisons, explosives, sanitary or medical products, and toys. Some states also prohibit home-based businesses from making food, drink, or clothing. Disgruntled neighbors can be the source of complaints.

INVENTORY MANAGEMENT

If your business includes a ship's store or other method of product sales, add the following questions to the checklist:

- Have you selected your inventory?
- Have you found reliable suppliers who will assist you in the start-up?
- Have you compared prices, quality, and credit terms of suppliers?
- Have you made a plan based upon estimated sales to determine the replacement purchases you will need for inventory turnover? (See chapter 2.)

REGULATIONS, LICENSES, ZONING, PERMITS, AND TAXES

Although exact regulations for businesses will vary from state to state, certain general requirements will have to be met. The chamber of commerce or the local small business administration office can provide specific information. A telephone call or a visit to the city and county licensing and zoning departments can also help avoid confusion.

When applying for a license, pay attention to the terminology you use to describe the potential business. For example, the license needed to run a bait shop that rents out johnboats can be much less costly than a license for operating a fishing guide and charter service. When making queries, be circumspect. General requirements follow.

City and County

You will need a business license from one entity, or perhaps both. A business license serves two purposes: (1) It gives the operator legal authority to conduct business; (2) if the business is making little or no profit, a license is one indicator to the IRS that the operator is truly in business, rates business write-offs, and is not merely pursuing a hobby.

State

The state might require that you file for a sales and use tax number. You should also obtain appropriate publications for filing state income and unemployment taxes and disability or medical taxes if appropriate. If the business is not a corporation, and you are doing business under a name not your own, you will have to register for a fictitious name (as mentioned earlier), either with the state or county.

Federal

Contact the IRS for a business tax kit. This will include forms and publications for your particular business entity. It also will explain procedures for obtaining an employer's identification number (EIN) and for paying estimated income tax, social security and medicare (FICA) taxes, and Federal Unemployment Tax Act (FUTA) taxes. Most businesses need an EIN whether or not they hire employees. A sole proprietorship will probably need an EIN only if it hires employees.[12]

In addition to preparing business tax kits, some IRS offices periodically hold small business seminars. Phone the local IRS number to enquire about dates and places.

Charter operators can also obtain assistance for federal income tax planning from two books written by specialists: *Tax Guide for the Business Use of Yachts*, by Mike Kimball, CPA, Roger A. Smith, CPA, and Dr. Karen S. Lee, J.D., CPA; and *Tax Guide for the Business Use of Yachts, Volume II: Charter Operations*, by Kimball and Smith. See notes for how to order them.[13]

INDEPENDENT CONTRACTORS AS CAPTAIN AND CREW

You sometimes can avoid employee costs such as social security and unemployment taxes by using independent contractors as captains and crew members.

However, if the IRS should someday reclassify one of your contractors from contractor to common-law employee, you could wind up paying all those costs anyway, as well as shelling out a stiff fine. Even if the IRS does not audit your tax returns, you never know when a disgruntled former skipper or crew member might file a complaint. Therefore, you should be aware of what the IRS considers a common-law employee and take positive steps to keep independent contractors independent.[14]

According to the IRS, a common-law employee is under the "direction and control" of the business. The services performed are subject to the will of an owner or an owner's employee of the business. The common-law employee is not just told what to do, but also is told how, when, and where it is to be done. Furthermore, he or she is provided a place to perform the services and is given the tools, equipment, supplies, and workers needed to do the job.

Obviously, you cannot treat an independent contractor as described above. You should confirm this with a written agreement. The agreement should spell out the job to be performed, state the fact that the contractor is not to be treated as an employee for federal tax purposes, state the duration of the agreement, and outline the amount and payment schedule of any compensation. You might stipulate that the contractor may hire and supervise subcontractors at the contractor's expense. If appropriate, the agreement should specify that the contractor provide the tools and supplies.

Additionally, your company should file all necessary income tax returns (including 1099-MISC forms to report amounts over $600 per year to each independent contractor). In case of audit, you should be prepared to provide a reasonable basis for not treating an independent contractor as an employee. You could derive such "reasonable basis" from any of the following:

- Judicial precedent, published rulings, technical advice memos, or letter rulings to your company.
- A past determination by the IRS in an examination that a person holding a substantially similar position was properly treated as a nonemployee.
- A long-standing known industry practice of treating such workers as independent contractors, which has not been unilaterally challenged by the IRS.

When possible, review your plans in advance with your accountant.

SUMMARY

1. Aptitude and learning offer the best combination for success in a charter business or any business.

2. Successful marketing depends upon finding out what the customers want and giving it to them in a way that no competitor can beat or equal. When you can do that at a profit, you have found a business niche.
3. Your final predeparture checklist includes the following:
   Your business first mates (accountant, attorney, and lender).
   Your business entity.
   Your business name.
   Your business location.
   Inventory management.
   Regulations, licenses, zoning, permits, and taxes.
   Accounting and budgeting (see chapter 2).
   Liability (see chapter 3).
   Marketing (see chapters 4 and 5)
   Your business plan (see chapter 6).
   Financing (see chapter 6).

CHAPTER 2

Accounting and Budgeting

KEEPING FINANCIAL RECORDS

On payday, a professional captain deposits his check in the Seaman's Bank and withdraws part of the total. He stops by The Old Watering Hole and buys himself a drink and one for his buddy. He springs for two boiled-lobster dinners and another round of drinks. Then he leaves The Old Watering Hole with enough cash left to pay his rent, buy gas for his pickup truck, and pay for enough groceries to last until the next payday. He climbs into his truck and heads for home, happy that his checking account balance remains large enough to handle short-term emergencies, and that his savings account nest egg is growing.

The captain has just performed a basic accounting cycle, much like many of us do every day. He knew how much money he had on hand and in the bank, and he budgeted his income and expenses. He also had a handle on long-term assets and possible liabilities.

Most charter operators must handle their accounting more formally, simply because business transactions get too complicated to remember.[1] They don't have to operate as CPAs; that's why they have accountants. But they do have to keep fairly detailed accounting records so that they or their accountants can take the following actions:

1. Prepare income tax and other required financial returns.
2. Prepare financial statements that will portray the health of the business.

These financial statements should answer the questions, "How much cash do I expect to have on hand?" "When should I break even?" "How much profit did I make?" and "What do I own and how much do I owe?" They will be integral parts of your financial plan, which should be a full chapter in the business plan (see chapter 6). The figures they contain will describe your business financially to anybody interested, such as your accountant, your attorney, potential lenders, possible buyers, the Internal Revenue Service, and, above all, *you.*

To start keeping records as a charter operator, you will have to make three decisions to fit your particular operation. You need to determine an *accounting period*, an *accounting method*,[2] and a systematic way to record your accounting—a method of *bookkeeping*.

Accounting Periods

Records can be summarized monthly, seasonally, annually, or at any other time. However, the IRS requires that each business prepare returns on a tax-year basis. Thus, it is generally simpler to dovetail business accounting periods with the IRS tax year. A tax year can be a calendar year, a fiscal year, or a "short tax year."

A calendar year, obviously, runs from January 1 through December 31. A fiscal year can be any consecutive twelve-month period ending on the last day of any month except December. It also might be a "52-53 week year" if the charter operator closes the accounts, say, the first Monday in September. A seasonal charter business might operate on a fiscal year or 52-53-week-year basis, with the year ending at the close of the season.

A short tax year is a tax year of fewer than twelve months; this occurs if the business is not in existence for an entire tax year or if it changes its tax year. Although the tax laws are continually being modified, here are some general guidelines:

- Businesses that do not maintain a set of books and records must use the calendar year.
- Sole proprietors must use the same tax year as their personal tax year, unless the IRS grants permission to do otherwise.
- In a partnership where the principal partners (those having an interest of 5 percent or more in partnership profits or capital) do not all have the same tax year, an IRS counselor or an accountant should be consulted.
- Any service corporation formed January 1, 1988, or later must use the calendar year.
- S corporations must use the calendar year unless the corporation can establish a business purpose for having a different tax year.
- Corporations that are not service corporations establish their tax year when they file their first income tax return. For example, the filing of a calendar year return or a short-tax-year return ending on December 31 establishes a calendar tax year for a corporation.

Accounting Methods

Do you wish to account for income when you earn it or when you receive it? Do you want to account for expenses when they are due or when you pay them? The answers help determine which accounting method you use—cash or accrual.

Most smaller businesses find it simpler to use the cash method. With this method, you include in your gross income all items of income (including property and services) you actually or constructively receive during the year. (Income received constructively is income credited to your account or made available to you without restriction as to the time and manner of payment.)

If you use the cash method of deducting expenses, you usually are expected to deduct them in the tax year in which you pay them. However, expenses you pay in advance can be deducted only in the year in which they apply.

Under the accrual method, all items of income are included in your gross income when you earn them, even though you may receive payment in another tax year. Expenses are deducted when you incur them, whether or not you pay them in the same year.

Bookkeeping

Unlike the professional skipper mentioned at the beginning of this chapter who kept his accounts in his head, most charter operators have to do their accounting on paper. They need a bookkeeping system, which can be either single- or double-entry. A single-entry system is the simplest to maintain, while a double-entry system can assure accuracy and control over larger charter operations because of built-in checks and balances.

Single-entry bookkeeping accounts for the flow of income and expenses through the use of daily and monthly summaries of cash receipts and a monthly summary of disbursements. Thus, in the simplest form, a beginning bank balance, plus income, minus checks written, should equal the new bank balance.

In double-entry bookkeeping, transactions are first entered in a journal and then are posted to ledger accounts. Each account has a left side for debits and a right side for credits. The system is self-balancing because every transaction is recorded as a debit entry in one account and as a credit entry in another. Thus, after the journal entries are posted to the ledger accounts, the total of the amounts entered as debits must equal the total of the amounts entered as credits. An imbalance in accounts indicates an error, which can then be found and corrected.

As mentioned in chapter 7 on computer assistance, accounting software for your computer can greatly simplify bookkeeping. Software will lead you through the required steps, do the calculations automatically and accurately, and provide financial statements you need with the tap of a key. It might even copy your figures into a program for income tax return preparation, chopping hours off the old, mistake-prone, manual systems used in the past.

Even a simple computer spreadsheet can save time and drudgery and eliminate inaccuracy, while giving you graphical analyses of your business (see chapter 7 for ideas).

A Basic Accounting System

An operator of a large charter business might have a separate accounting department, complete with dedicated computers and associated software, busy making daily closeouts and balances and producing massive printouts for each division. However, if you are an operator of a smaller business, you might collect accounting information as transactions occur, manually sort it by category, and convert it into financial statements once a month. You can process it either via a manual system or through a simple spreadsheet system that you set up yourself. Think of collecting everything in two shoe boxes, like this:

Box 1—Income. Use a receipt book for all income received. Record categories of income on the receipts, such as "charter fee," or "soft drink sales." Transfer all money from the box to a business checking account. Keep the receipts in the box until time for preparing financial statements.

Box 2—Outgo. Write checks from the business bank account for all expenses, and annotate categories of expenditures, such as "fuel" or "loan payment," on the stubs or copies. Attach to the corresponding stubs or copies any bills and statements received. Keep all of this in the box until time for preparing financial statements.

The result is basic single-entry bookkeeping, with each transaction documented: The beginning bank balance, plus income, minus checks written, equals the new bank balance. The categorized amounts of income and outgo become the basis of the financial statements.

FINANCIAL STATEMENTS AND OTHER RECORDS

Whether you do your accounting with two boxes or via a more complicated method, you can use the results to answer those important questions listed earlier. A *monthly cash-flow statement* (or cash projection) will show how much cash you expect to have at the end of each month. A *three-year income projection* will show your estimated profits (or losses) for three years. *Break-even analysis* will disclose how much you must sell under varying scenarios to break even. A *profit-and-loss statement* (or income statement) will show how much profit you made in a specified period. And a *balance sheet* (or net worth statement) will reveal what you own and how much you owe as of the date of the statement.

Each of these has a place in the business plan. Let's take a look at these and other records vital to your business's success.

Monthly Cash-Flow Statement (Cash Projection)

If you are going to owe $10,000 at the end of seven months but you expect to net $10,000 in charter fees by that time, you're in good shape, right? Not if you earn all the charter fees during the seventh month and must bill them to your customers' thirty-day credit accounts. A monthly cash-flow statement will foresee such problems and compensate for them.

For instance, if you must pay dockage semiannually, your cash projection might allow for several monthly accumulations of cash to cover the lump-sum payment. You also might accumulate funds for annual haul-out fees—or, conversely, make arrangements with the yard for monthly billings. In another example, if your chartering business is seasonal, the cash-flow statement can ensure that you will have funds for fixed expenses that occur during the off-season.

Figure 2-1 is a basic monthly cash-flow statement format that can be modified to fit the financial records of your business. It should have columns that run through a twelve-month period, which can be prepared easily on a

JANUARY		
	Estimated	*Actual*
BEGINNING CASH	$10,000	$10,000
CASH RECEIPTS		
Charter revenues	5,000	4,000
Marina income	2,000	500
Credit collections	1,000	500
CASH PAID OUT		
Office	1,000	1,000
Boat	2,000	2,000
Capital purchases	1,000	1,500
Owner's withdrawal	2,000	1,500
ENDING CASH	$12,000	$9,000

Figure 2-1. ABC Chartering Company—monthly cash flow statement

computer spreadsheet program. The ending cash-flow total should equal your business bank balance and any other cash belonging to the business.

Remember that a cash-flow statement shows *cash* only and is only indirectly connected with profits and losses. Estimated *profits and losses* will be forecast in the three-year income projection and actual profits and losses will be disclosed by the profit-and-loss statement, both discussed below.

Looking at figure 2-1, let's assume that Captain Charterman starts the year with $10,000 in cash, so his estimated and actual beginning cash totals are the same. Let's also say that he wants to have $9,000 in cash for a major bill in February. To keep his cash at $9,000, he decides to withdraw only $1,500 for his compensation. He is not concerned about the actual cash flow being lower than estimated because he will have additional marina income of $2,000 on credit from long-term customers who always pay within thirty days.

Three-Year Income Projection

A simple three-year income projection can be created by using the following components:

- Estimated profits.
- Expected sales, including charter contracts, as well as ancillary sales of items such as ship's store merchandise, fuel, ice, and bait.
- Fixed expenses—the costs of staying in business, regardless of whether a boat is ever let out to charter. Examples are insurance, rent, dock fees, property taxes, wages paid to full-time employees, boat depreciation, loan interest, office expenses, and scheduled maintenance.
- Variable expenses—costs that vary with the business volume. For instance, an increase in crewed charters can boost employee wages, whereas an increase in bareboat charters might add unscheduled maintenance costs. A change in the volume or types of advertising will cause that line item to vary. And adding live-bait tanks will create "cost of bait sold" as a variable expense.

Although sales, minus fixed and variable expenses, equals profit, other formulas can simplify projection brainstorming. For example, subtracting variable expenses from sales provides a fifth component, which we'll call *income*. For the projection to balance, income should equal fixed expenses plus profit. Let's look at part 1 of figure 2-2, which shows a projection with sales of $30,000, variable expenses of $16,000, and fixed expenses of $5,000.

The profit will be $9,000. Now go to part 2 of figure 2-2 to see how much sales would have to increase in order to double the profit. Assuming that fixed

PART 1			
Sales	30,000	Fixed expenses	5,000
Variable expenses	- 16,000	Profit	+ ?,???
Income	14,000	Income	14,000
PART 2			
Sales	??,???	Fixed expenses	5,000
Variable expenses	- ??,???	Profit	+ 18,000
Income	23,000	Income	23,000
PART 3			
Sales	49,220	Fixed expenses	5,000
Variable expenses	- 26,220	Profit	+ 18,000
Income	23,000	Income	23,000

Figure 2-2. Projection brainstorming

expenses remain the same and variable expenses maintain the same ratio to sales, then sales must still be 214 percent of income. 214 percent × $23,000 = $49,220. Hence, part 3 of figure 2-2 shows sales at $49,220 and variable expenses of $26,220.

At this stage, Captain Charterman can evaluate how he might increase sales to $49,220. If the total number of charter days he expects to sell for the season won't support this increase, he can consider increasing charter fees. And he needs to look carefully at the variable expenses. If, for example, he can find a way to reduce variable expenses by $25 per charter day, and he expects 165 charter days for the season, he will increase income by $4,125, which increases profits dollar for dollar.

You can start a projection either by forecasting sales and working down, or by forecasting profits and working up. Using the system shown, once you have considered all possibilities, if income equals fixed expenses plus profit, the projection is doable.

A year-end financial summary will offer a chance to fine-tune that year's projection as a planning tool for the next year. For a start, the summary will show you whether the present profit is large enough to provide a return on investment and give you a salary for your work. At that point, you should be careful about concluding, "I'm satisfied, because the business made my boat payments and fed me last year." As sure as Neptune lives in the sea, if that's *all* the business does for you, you need to establish a better projection, or consider employment that will pay for the boat, feed you, *and* pay you a salary.

As your business grows, you might need other types of budget projections, such as projections for expenses, administrative expenses, an income statement, or a projection of collections of accounts receivable.

Break-even Analysis

Break-even is the point at which gross profit equals expenses. In a business year, it is the time at which sales volume has become sufficient to enable the overall operation to start showing a profit. Preparation of the analysis, which can be done either mathematically or graphically, is simplified by the use of computer spreadsheet software. You can use the following steps to determine the break-even point and obtain a budgeted sales price (charter fee).

Estimate the number of charter days you expect per month (or for the season). Divide expenses by charter days. If weather, maintenance, or other variables can interfere, use 75 percent or 80 percent of estimated charter days (or whatever percentage you feel is the most likely). The result is the break-even price per day.

For actual charter price per day, add desired (or estimated possible) net profit to expenses, and divide by charter days.

Figure 2-3 provides another example of break-even analysis. In statement A of figure 2-3, the sales volume is at the break-even point and there is no profit. In statement B for the same charter operation, the sales volume is beyond the break-even point and a profit is shown. In the two statements, the percentage factors are the same except for fixed expenses, total expenses, and operating profit.

Figure 2-3 shows that, once sales volume reaches the break-even point, fixed expenses are covered. Beyond the break-even point, every dollar of sales should earn an equivalent additional profit percentage.

Looking at it another way, once sales pass the break-even point, the fixed expenses percentage goes down as the sales volume goes up. And the operating profit percentage increases at the same rate as the percentage rate for fixed expenses decreases, as long as variable expenses are kept in line. In figure 2-3, fixed expenses in statement B decreased by 5 percent and operating profit increased by 5 percent.

Profit-and-Loss Statement (P&L)

The P&L presents a summary of the financial transactions of the business during a stated period, whether it be a month, six months, or a year. It indicates: (1) the income earned from chartering fees, from merchandise sales if any, and from any other source connected with the business; (2) all expenses incurred during the period; and (3) the net result in form of profit earned or loss incurred for the period.

But the P&L goes beyond merely listing income, expenses, and the difference. It offers a chance to compare operations against the previous period or periods. It also provides a tool for obtaining the most efficiency from the expense dollar by analyzing and subsequently reducing expenses. And it can

	A		B	
	Break-even Amount	*Percent of Sales*	*Profit Amount*	*Percent of Sales*
Sales	50,000	100	60,000	100
Cost of sales	30,000	60	36,000	60
Gross profit	20,000	40	24,000	40
OPERATING EXPENSES				
Fixed	15,000	30	15,000	25
Variable	5,000	10	6,000	10
Total	20,000	40	21,000	35
Operating profit	None	0	3,000	5

Figure 2-3. Break-even analysis

show how to maximize profits by combining sales volume with cost control. In short, it tells you where you are, and how you got there, and gives you a good idea of how you're doing.

Some aspects of the financial picture of a charter operation may be as obvious as a 15-degree list. The hypothetical ABC Chartering Company's annual P&L, shown in figure 2-4, provides several examples.

An accountant might analyze ABC's P&L as follows: To begin with, the year's net profit of $3,600 does not warrant the time and effort that Captain Charterman is contributing, unless he is in business just to pay for his boat. In that case, he paid $2,250 in interest, apparently for a loan, and has $3,600 available to repay principal and to eat.

Captain Charterman should analyze his low profit figures by breaking down sales and expenses into two categories: merchandise and charter fees. Then he can compare expenses as percentages of sales for each category, as shown in figure 2-5.

Looking at figure 2-5, let's say that the $1,500 loss on merchandise sales occurred because the operator did not price his inventory properly. He received a 30 percent discount when he bought the items, but sold them at barely more than cost, perhaps believing that the ship's store would carry itself while drawing charter customers. He should have set the sales price—provided competition allowed it—at $34,286 ($24,000 divided by 70 percent equals $34,286) instead of $25,000. This markup price would have covered costs and would have given a net profit of $7,786 ($10,286 minus operating expenses of $2,500).

Now look at the other trouble spot. More than 57 percent of the charter fee income is spent for payroll, and that does not include the charter operator's

GROSS SALES		70,000
COST OF SALES:		
Opening inventory	13,000	
Purchases	25,000	
Total	38,000	
Ending inventory	14,000	
TOTAL COST OF SALES		24,000
GROSS PROFIT		46,000
OPERATING EXPENSES:		
Payroll (not including owner)	26,000	
Dock and office rental	3,000	
Payroll taxes	1,500	
Interest	2,250	
Depreciation	5,250	
Telephone	2,400	
Insurance	1,000	
Miscellaneous	1,000	
TOTAL OPERATING EXPENSES		42,400
NET PROFIT (before owner's salary)		3,600

Figure 2-4. Profit-and-loss statement: ABC Chartering Company

salary. Therefore, the operator needs either to increase charter fees or to make more efficient use of the employees.

Is he passing payroll costs for his captains through to the customers? Is he paying charter wages to his captains even when they are between charters? Is he paying excessive wages out of loyalty to employees? Should he pay by the hour, the job, or the month? Does he often find himself sitting in a deserted ship's store while he's paying an employee to take a boat somewhere? The $2,300 telephone bill charged against charter fees also needs a review. Since there is no advertising cost, maybe he uses the telephone to draw customers. If so, perhaps he can find a way to advertise through the mail and reduce long-distance telephone calls.

If the ship's store operation is to continue, the average inventory might be cut in order to free up some operating funds. The average inventory for the

ABC CHARTERING COMPANY	TOTAL		MERCHANDISE		CHARTER FEES	
	Amount	*%*	*Amount*	*%*	*Amount*	*%*
GROSS SALES	70,000	100.00	25,000	100.00	45,000	100.00
COST OF SALES						
Opening inventory	13,000		13,000			
Purchases	25,000		25,000			
Total	38,000		38,000			
Ending inventory	14,000		14,000			
TOTAL COST OF SALES	24,000	34.29	24,000	96.00		
GROSS PROFIT	46,000	65.71	1,000	4.00		
OPERATING EXPENSES						
Payroll (not including owner)	26,000	37.14			26,000	57.78
Dock and office rental	3,000	4.29	1,500	6.00	1,500	3.33
Payroll taxes	1,500	2.14			1,500	3.33
Interest	2,250	3.21			2,250	5.00
Depreciation	5,250	7.50			5,250	11.68
Telephone	2,400	3.43	100	.40	2,300	5.11
Insurance	1,000	1.43	400	1.60	600	1.33
Miscellaneous	1,000	1.43	500	2.00	500	1.11
TOTAL OPERATING EXPENSES	42,400	60.57	2,500	10.00	39,900	88.67
NET PROFIT (not including owner's salary)	3,600	5.14	(1,500)	(6.00)	5,100	11.33

Figure 2-5. Profit-and-loss statement: expenses as percentages of sales

twelve-month period is $13,500 ($13,000 opening inventory, $14,000 ending inventory, average inventory $13,500). With the cost of sales being $24,000, the average inventory was used less than twice a year. To put it another way, the ending inventory of $14,000 represents a ship's store supply for approximately seven months.

Knowing this, the charter operator might find ways to reduce the average inventory. Inventory control measures and comparison of unit costs can disclose which items to stock in greater quantities than others. A survey of distributors might result in arrangements for immediate delivery of some items, thus greatly reducing the need for in-store inventory.

This example of ABC Chartering Company shows the need for using percentages for analysis. If you increase sales and retain the dollar amount of an expense, you have decreased the expense as a percentage of sales. When you decrease your cost percentage, you increase your percentage of profit.

On the other hand, if sales volume remains the same, you can increase the percentage of profit by reducing a specific item of expense. Your goal, of course, is to do both: to decrease specific expenses and increase their productive worth at the same time.

Balance Sheet (Net Worth Statement)

The balance sheet is a listing of all assets (money and property owned by the business) and all liabilities (debts outstanding). The mathematical difference between the two is net worth. In basic terms, if a charter operator is about to go out of business, the balance sheet will reveal whether there are enough current assets to pay off current liabilities—whether the business can pay its bills. However, the balance sheet can be used for more sophisticated evaluations, as will be shown. Figure 2-6 contains a balance sheet for a sole proprietorship.

Here are definitions for the terms used in figure 2-6.

Current assets. Cash and other assets that can be converted to cash in a relatively short period. In the example shown, where ninety days is used, the charter operator probably expects to turn over the ship's store merchandise within that period.

Cash. Money on hand, in the till, or on deposit in a bank.

Accounts receivable. Money owed to the business and still unpaid as of the date of the balance sheet. If the $5,000 in the example is for ship's store merchandise sold by credit card, the operator is probably shipshape and watertight. If it represents signed charter contracts that are to be executed in the next ninety days, the operator could be riding in a leaky boat.

Inventory. Merchandise for sale, in this case from the operator's ship's store and fuel dock.

Fixed assets (also called long-term, or slow, assets). These include assets, such as the boat in the example, that probably could not be sold quickly for cash. A slow account receivable might also be shown as a fixed asset.

Current liabilities. Debts which are due for payment in a relatively short period. In the example in figure 2-6, ninety days is used to balance against the ninety-day period established for current assets. The charter operator has multiplied the monthly boat loan payment, dock fee, and insurance premium by three to obtain the totals shown.

ASSETS		LIABILITIES	
Current Assets		*Current Liabilities*	
Cash	5,000	Accounts payable	6,000
Accounts receivable	5,000	Boat loan	1,200
Inventory	5,000	Dockage	900
		Insurance	600
Total current assets	15,000	Total current liabilities	8,700
Fixed Assets		*Fixed Liabilities*	
Boat	40,000	Boat loan	35,000
		Net worth	11,300
Total fixed assets	40,000	Total fixed liabilities	46,300
Total assets	55,000	Total liabilities	55,000

Figure 2-6. Balance sheet for sole proprietorship

Accounts payable. This is money owed to others. Although the charter operator knows what accounts these are, a loan officer or a prospective buyer of the business would want to know what this $6,000 represents. For example, if it is merchandise or fuel, the operator is probably more stable financially than if it is a bill for a recent haulout.

Fixed liabilities (also called long-term, or slow, liabilities). These are debts that the owner will probably not have to repay for a long period. In the example, the balance due on the boat loan as of the date of the balance sheet is shown as a fixed liability.

Net worth. This $11,300 was obtained by subtracting all other liabilities from total assets.

Working capital. One of the most important concepts of the balance sheet is the distinction between *working capital* and *capital.* Working capital is the difference between current assets ($15,000) and current liabilities ($8,700). After paying the bills shown, the charter operator has $6,300 for reserves, contingencies, improvements to the business, and personal pay.

Current ratio. This is current assets divided by current liabilities. A ratio of 2:1 is generally considered good, while 1.5:1 is sometimes acceptable. The current ratio in the example is 1.7:1. The dollar value of working capital can also indicate that the business is a good risk for a short-term unsecured loan.

Capital. The term capital, on the other hand, represents the owner's total equity in both current and fixed assets, which in this case is net worth, or

$11,300. If he obtained his boat with a $4,000 down payment, then his net worth has increased. If he has withdrawn capital in the past, then he is prospering. However, if the estimated market value of his boat, shown as $40,000, is inflated, he might be deluding himself as to the true extent of his capital.

Liquid Assets. If there is any question about whether the inventory will turn over in ninety days, the owner (and prospective lender) needs to consider liquid assets as being only cash and accounts receivable (assuming accounts receivable is viable). In the example, cash and accounts receivable total $10,000, which is more than enough to pay total current liabilities of $8,700, so the owner is still in a comfortable position. Conversely, if liquid assets were only $5,000 and current liabilities were still $8,700, the operator would be headed toward shoal water.

Goodwill. Goodwill is an intangible asset whose exact value can be determined only if the business is sold. A lender will seldom accept goodwill as collateral. If goodwill shows up in the balance sheet, it should be deducted from the book value of net worth in order to obtain a total *tangible net worth*. In the example shown, if a buyer pays the owner more than the business's net worth of $11,300, it could be an investment in anticipated future profits, or a payment for goodwill, or both.

Balance Sheets for Businesses That Are Not Sole Proprietorships

Figure 2-6 represents a balance sheet for a sole proprietorship. If the business were a 50-50 partnership, net worth could be shown on two separate lines as $5,650 for each partner. Other partnership ratios would be shown accordingly. A corporate balance sheet would list *capital stock* and *surplus* as fixed liabilities. Their sum would be corporate net worth. Another line, *reserve for federal income tax*, would be added as a short-term liability. That line is not needed for proprietorships, partnerships, and S corporations, because they generally pay no federal income tax (see chapter 1).

Your Business Bank Account

You should have a separate, business bank account for your chartering business. If you commingle funds (like shoving a charter fee into your pocket, then using it to pay your personal grocery bill), your records can become meaningless. Such sloppy accounting can lead the IRS to suspect you of hiding profits, on the one hand, or merely operating a hobby (thus making you ineligible for certain business write-offs), on the other. A separate bank account avoids these problems and provides the machinery for the basic accounting arithmetic cited earlier: Bank balance, plus income, minus checks written, equals new bank balance. Be sure to reconcile the account upon receipt of each bank statement.

(Ensure that your record of bank balance is the same as the bank's as of the day of the statement.)

Petty Cash

Even with a business bank account, many expenses will have to be paid by cash. Failure to control and record these miscellaneous monies can bilge the bookkeeping system before it even gets under way.

For several years while I was in secondary school, I worked part time as a newspaper carrier and collected payments from my customers once a month. Under my contract with the newspaper office, I would use the first funds collected to pay for the papers (the overhead) and keep the remainder as profit. Before starting to collect, I would withdraw $10 in nickels, dimes, and quarters from my bank account, to be sure I could make change. Each evening during collections week I would treat myself at a bakery located along the route, paying from the ditty bag full of change. My monthly profits always seemed to come up about $10 short.

I wasn't handling my petty-cash account properly and thus was stealing from my business and reducing profits. There are two ways to avoid such an outcome in a chartering business:

1. Cash a check for a minimum usable amount—say $50. Keep the money in a separate box from the cash in the register drawer. As money is needed, withdraw it from the petty-cash box and replace it with a receipt. Thus, at all times the petty-cash box contains $50 in cash and receipts. If you remove money for personal purposes, mark a petty cash receipt "DRAW," and place it in the petty-cash box. When the cash on hand runs low, total the receipts by *category* (i.e., office supplies, tolls, and so forth). Write a check payable to petty cash for the total amount of the receipts, and list the categories and amounts on the stub. The petty-cash fund now has $50 cash on hand.
2. The second approach works well for a charter operator on the run. Pay for miscellaneous purchases out of pocket, and place receipts in a box or other container. Occasionally, or perhaps once a month, sort out the receipts by category and write yourself a check, annotating the stub with the categories and amounts. With this method, the business is never out a penny, and the accounting is as secure as a double-clamped hose.

Payroll

You must make periodical reports of individual payroll payments to state and federal governments. Additionally, you must provide each employee with a

W-2 form at year's end, showing total withholding payments you made during the calendar year.

In order to prepare such reports, you should keep an employment card for each employee, showing social security number, name, address, telephone number, name and address of next of kin, whether the employee is married, and the number of exemptions claimed. Use a separate sheet for the employee's individual payroll record, listing rate of pay, social security number, amounts for each pay period covering hours worked, gross pay, and the deductions.

Taxes

Establish a system to ensure that accurate taxes and associated reports will be made on time to the state and federal governments. See chapter 1 for more information on tax planning.

Do not overlook the requirement for estimated tax payments. Anyone who receives income that hasn't been subject to withholding, or whose withholding isn't enough, may be required to pay estimated taxes four times per year. Failure to do so may result in a penalty even if you are due a refund when you file your income tax return.[3]

Accounts Receivable

If you carry credit for your customers, here are guidelines to help you keep them under control. Although some of these might appear simple, failure to observe each one has forced more than one company to go under.

- Make sure that credit is warranted before you grant it.
- Be sure bills are prepared and mailed to correct addresses.
- "Age" your accounts receivable at the end of each month by arranging each account in one of three categories: current, unpaid for thirty days, or sixty days and over. Find out why all accounts for sixty days and over are unpaid.
- Listen carefully to customers' complaints about bills. If a complaint is justified, propose an adjustment to the customer and make it promptly.
- If a customer is delinquent, try to obtain a promise of payment on a definite date. If you don't receive it on that date, ask the customer to explain why and get a new promise.

As you age the accounts, ask yourself questions like these: Have some already been pledged to another creditor? What is the accounts receivable turnover? Is the total weakened because many customers are far behind in their payments? Have you established a reserve large enough to cover doubtful accounts? How much do the largest accounts owe and what percentage of the total accounts does this amount represent? Does the accounts receivable include anticipated seasonal or return charterers? If so, are these covered by contracts? With deposits? By customer history? With reserves for adverse weather, airline strikes, or other unforeseen events?

Equipment and Depreciation

Keep a list of permanent equipment used in the business. These are items of depreciable value that are useful for longer than a year, such as the boat or boats, cars, trucks, tools, furniture, and fixtures. You will need to record the description, date purchased, and purchase price. You can then use the list as the basis for calculating depreciation and providing data for the fixed asset section of the balance sheet.

Logs

We're not talking about deck logs or engineering logs. We're talking about logs the IRS insists a charter operator keep for use of a vehicle or a computer part time in the business. If you should claim automobile expense mileage, for instance, and can't produce a log, the IRS could label the entry fraudulent, as opposed to merely disallowing the claim. Keep your log at or near the location where the use takes place.

For a vehicle, keeping a simple form under the seat to record business use of the vehicle can be an easy solution. It might have columns headed as shown in figure 2-7.

TIME				MILEAGE (Odometer Readings)			
Date	*Start*	*Finish*	*Total*	*Begin*	*End*	*Total*	*Notes*

Figure 2-7. Mileage log

Date	*Activity*	*Time Started*	*Time Finished*	*Business or Personal*	*Notes*

Figure 2-8. Computer log

For a computer, the log should show times of personal use as well as times of business use. It could be kept near the computer or could be recorded in a computer file. A computer log might be set up as shown in figure 2-8.

SUMMARY

This summary is an outline of the topics covered, in order to assist in organizing or reorganizing your own accounting and bookkeeping system. You can use it as a checklist and a basis from which to build your own system. A charter operator who takes the time to plan record keeping and analyze financial statements will give thanks every time he or she goes to the bank.

Keeping Financial Records
- Accounting Periods
- Accounting Methods
- Bookkeeping
- A Basic Accounting System
  - Box 1 - Income
  - Box 2 - Outgo
- Results

Financial Statements and Other Records
- Monthly Cash-Flow Statement (Cash Projection)
- Three-Year Income Projection
- Break-even Analysis
- Profit-and-Loss Statement
- Balance Sheet (Net Worth Statement)
- Definitions
- Balance Sheets for Businesses That Are Not Sole Proprietorships
- Your Business Bank Account
- Petty Cash
- Payroll
- Taxes
- Accounts Receivable
- Equipment and Depreciation
- Logs

CHAPTER 3

How to Prepare an Insurance Plan

From the day you form your company until the day you leave it, you must overcome risks to achieve success. As a marketer, you expect to convert marketplace risk into profits by following a logically prepared marketing plan. As part of that marketing plan, you determine how to manage the risks of property loss, loss of business income, and liability loss. The result is an insurance plan that becomes a separate chapter in the marketing plan.

You can manage risks in three ways: (1) eliminate or reduce them, (2) transfer them to an insurer, or (3) accept them.[1] To make your decision, first you must evaluate the risks, both shoreside and marine.

PROPERTY LOSS

The Physical Plant. Study your buildings, plate-glass windows, glass display cases, furniture, computers, and other office appliances. Review your inventory and warehousing for the ship's store or the dive shop. Consider the volume and locations of your administrative records, your computer disks, and any cash stored in the office. Then decide what the loss of each would mean to your business, and how you might manage that loss.

Vehicles. If you want collision insurance for automobiles and other vehicles used in the business, be sure to insure them for commercial use.

Home Office. If you use a computer, fax machine, or other office equipment at home in your chartering business, check your homeowner's policy to see if it covers such use.

Crime. Evaluate how vulnerable your business is to burglary, robbery, and vandalism. Consider your risk of receiving bad checks and credit cards. If your employees handle large sums of your money, decide whether they should be bonded.

LOSS OF BUSINESS INCOME

As a charter operator, you might require more life and health insurance (L&H) on yourself than you carried before you started the business. You also might need L&H for other key members of the business—perhaps for all of your employees.

What will happen to accounts receivable, accounts payable, and the charter operation in general if you should die or become disabled? Perhaps you need key-person insurance (in addition to or instead of L&H). And you might want to insure other key people in the company whose unexpected loss might precipitate a financial calamity.

LIABILITY

Most small business operators buy all the liability insurance they can afford. Such insurance can protect you in case of injury to an employee or customer, or in case of a malfunction associated with your products or services. Another must is workers' compensation insurance, to protect you from extensive common-law liability to your employees. Be sure your vehicles are covered for liability, and confirm that the employees who use them have current operator licenses.

MARINE PROPERTY LOSS

If you operate a fleet of outboard-powered runabouts near the interstate in Pennsylvania, your risk of theft is quite different than if you are chartering the only sailboat on Lake Tiny in West Texas, and the boat can be hauled only with your lift. Meanwhile, a fleet of sailboats chartering out of Oahu, Hawaii, face completely different risks of damage from sinking than does that sailboat on Lake Tiny. Evaluate the level of every risk to your boat (or fleet).

If you carry cargo for hire, include it in your insurance planning. And if you use personal property on your boat that you want to insure, such as dive gear or fishing equipment, find out if you need to cover the property with a commercial policy or endorsement.

LOSS OF MARINE BUSINESS INCOME

As the skipper of your charter boat, your license is at risk every time you cast off the dock lines. Your insurance plan should include the possibility of your license being surrendered, deposited, suspended, or revoked (see chapter 13).

You also should evaluate loss of income due to losing your license, or from bad publicity because of a vessel or personnel casualty. And what if your entire operation should be shut down by natural catastrophe? (Since *Charter Your Boat for Profit* was published in 1989, hurricanes have destroyed a vast number of chartering operations in the Caribbean and the Atlantic.)

MARINE LIABILITY

From a charter operator's point of view, maritime law is little different from any other law, except for the terminology. Barry M. Snyder, a personal-injury trial lawyer who holds a 100-ton master's license, says that the idea of maritime law being bizarre or crazy is "a mythology." "It's just not so," he says. "Maritime law, like all other law, is based on common sense." [2]

At sea, as on land, if an employee or visitor is injured, a court might find someone or something responsible—the victim, the employer, the boss, or the working conditions (the vessel). If the victim is not found responsible, then another person or persons (or the vessel) might be ordered to pay damages, and perhaps to pay a form of employee compensation.

Under such circumstances, a vessel might be treated somewhat like a person because it can be a source of funds through mortgage or sale. Let's see how this occurs; then we will consider a captain and an owner as other sources of funds.

Vessel Liability—Maritime Liens and Actions *In Rem* and How Liens Are Enforced

A maritime lien (a right of property) can be placed against a vessel, much as a real estate lien can be placed against a house.[3] To accommodate a boat's mobility, a maritime lien stays with her wherever she is, until the lien is resolved. If the lien is proven in court, the boat can be sold to satisfy or partially satisfy the lien. [4] The following is a basic listing of sources of maritime liens:

- Crew wages. This lien has first priority over all other claims. It can be placed by master, crew, or any category of employee described under the Jones Act (see below).
- Claims for collision, personal injury, and wrongful death under the general maritime law (below), maintenance and cure, and property damage due to negligence.
- Breach of a charter party, if the charter party has a contract that the owner fails to honor.
- Salvage. A salvage lien can be placed against the vessel and any cargo saved. A charter operator may subject the vessel to a salvage claim if the crew abandons her in the face of a marine peril, and an outside party

voluntarily brings her to a safe haven. A charter operator also might create a salvage claim if the boat is towed when in danger, or under dangerous conditions, even though captain and crew remain aboard.[5]
- The catchall. The Federal Maritime Lien Act[6] states that any "person furnishing repairs, supplies, towage, use of dry dock or marine railway, or other necessaries, to any vessel . . . shall have a maritime lien on the vessel." The term *other necessaries* has been held by the courts to mean virtually anything an operator might buy or order for the boat, such as pilotage, dockage, stevedoring services, marine surveys, local ship's chandlery items, and oil spill containment or cleanup services.

When a lien is placed against a vessel (and at certain other times) the boat can be seized and held for action *in rem*. The term *in rem* signifies action against the *thing* (the boat), as opposed to action *in personam* (against a person). Seizing a boat and holding it for action *in rem* is much like jailing a person; it ensures that the vessel will be available for a possible sentence. As will be shown, it even allows for the possibility of "bail."

A lien is foreclosed by the proceeding *in rem*. When the vessel is in the federal district where a verified complaint has been filed, and the district court approves a warrant, a U.S. marshal simply goes out and "arrests" the boat. The person with the complaint must provide a deposit to cover insurance costs and custodial keeper costs that will occur after the vessel's arrest. Except for certain offenses requiring sale of the vessel, the owner can post a bond and recover the vessel. You might avoid the bond if the claimant agrees to accept a *letter of undertaking*. This simpler procedure, which can be executed even before the vessel is arrested, is a legal guarantee that you will pay any judgment up to a specified amount upon completion of the litigation. A letter of undertaking is somewhat like being released on your own recognizance.

If the owner does not claim the vessel and obtain its release, or if the amount of claims outstanding exceeds the value of the vessel, the claimant can ask the court to sell the vessel. Contributing factors here are the claimant's costs of keeping the vessel and whether or not the vessel is deteriorating while under arrest (thus reducing the claimant's chance eventually to receive a full judgment).

If the boat is sold under court order, in a sale confirmed by the court as valid (reasonable advertisements followed by a bidding procedure designed to bring the best available price), the buyer will receive a lien-free title.

As a charter operator, you could find yourself confronting a lien against your boat or placing a lien against another's boat. In either case you should work closely with an attorney who is familiar with admiralty law. And when thinking of buying a used vessel, you should be aware that it could have an unrecorded maritime lien.

A protection against unrecorded liens, although not guaranteed, is to buy a documented vessel, after obtaining copies of the abstract of title and certificate of ownership from the Coast Guard (as described in chapter 8). An even more secure protection is the court-ordered sale, described above. As John C. Person, an admiralty attorney in New Orleans, said in an article in *WorkBoat Magazine*, "Maritime liens accumulate on a ship's hull like invisible barnacles and can only be scraped off at a marshal's sale." [7]

Owner Is Responsible for Seaworthiness

The law holds that it is an owner's absolute and nondelegable duty to provide a vessel that is fit for its intended purposes or the intended voyage. This makes the vessel and the owner liable in case of injury or death of a crew member due to unseaworthiness.[8] The owner is liable even if unseaworthiness occurs after the vessel leaves port, and regardless of notice or opportunity to correct the unseaworthy condition. However, the law does not hold the owner responsible for negligence of the injured person's fellow crew members.

The court can find full damages against the owner, less contributory negligence (partly the fault of the crew member), excepting damages already paid for medical care, maintenance, and cure (discussed below).

The Jones Act—Employer Is Responsible for Negligence

Under the Jones Act,[9] any seaman who, in the course of employment, suffers personal injury due to employer negligence may seek damages from his employer through a jury trial. (An estate also can sue, in case of death.)[10] Courts have held that the term *seaman* refers to master, licensed and unlicensed hands, as well as bartenders, musicians, maids, and stewards. Damages have been awarded for pain and suffering, loss of earnings, inability to lead a normal life, and medical expenses. (See, however, the section on maintenance and cure, below.)

If as owner you hire a captain who hires the crew, you may be responsible for the crew. Conversely, if you put a boat into bareboat charter, a party that charters it and hires a captain or crew may become liable (see chapter 9 for an explanation of how a charter party becomes an owner).

Maintenance and Cure—Employer, Vessel, and Master Are Responsible

Maintenance and cure (M&C)[11] is like workers' compensation, in that negligence or unseaworthiness is not a factor. With certain exceptions for vessels under 18 net tons, a seaman (or the estate) can seek M&C if the seaman is injured or taken ill in the course of employment. The seaman can assert the claim against the employer, the vessel, and the master. The M&C can be for unearned wages, subsistence, and/or medical care. A seaman's lien for M&C will take priority over a mortgage lien against the vessel.

A seaman on shore leave (thus on call) when the injury or illness occurs probably will be considered to be in the course of employment. However, misconduct while on shore leave may deny an M&C settlement. (A vacation is not considered a shore leave.)

Owner Responsible for Noncrew Members

The law consistently holds that the owner has the duty of exercising reasonable care for anybody who is lawfully on board for purposes not inimical to the owner's legitimate interests and who are not members of the crew.[12] The findings include guests and others who are not crew members. The key word here is *reasonable care*.

The wording of the law is more strict when paying passengers are on board. In the case of *Moore v. American Scantic Line, Inc.*, the court affirmed that "A steamship company is not an 'insurer' of passengers' safety but owes the duty to exercise a very high degree of care for safety of passengers."[13] This "very high degree of care" forms the basis of the "Golden Rule of Liability" that is described in the section on eliminating or reducing risks (see page 56).

Contraband—Vessel and Owner Responsible

According to the law,[14] contraband is:

- Any narcotic drug that is possessed illegally, or that has been acquired, or is to be transferred illegally;
- Any narcotic drug that does not bear appropriate tax-paid internal revenue stamps; or
- Any firearm involved with a violation of the National Firearms Act.

Contraband can end a charter operation in a heartbeat, because federal authorities—and many state police officials—can seize any vessel involved with contraband. The law applies if contraband is aboard the boat or on the person of anybody aboard the boat. It also applies if the boat is used in any way to "facilitate the transportation, carriage, conveyance, concealment, receipt, possession, purchase, sale, barter, exchange or giving away" of any contraband article.

If contraband is proved in court, the seized vessel can be forfeited and sold, unless the owner can prove he or she had no knowledge of the contraband. If a charter party has the boat, the owner still might be required to prove he or she knew nothing about it. If the charter is a bareboat charter and the charter party is involved, the owner could lose the boat even if not personally involved (see chapter 9).

Pollution—Owner, Employer, Operator, and Vessel Responsible

Oil Pollution Act of 1990 (OPA 90). Passed in response to the *Exxon Valdez* grounding in Alaska, which spilled 11 million gallons of oil into Prince William Sound in March 1989, OPA 90 applies to all vessel owners and operators in U.S. waters. Under the law, an owner whose vessel spills enough oil or fuel to create a sheen on the surface of the water is in violation and could be fined. The owner or operator must take immediate action to limit liability, and the owner will be charged for all cleanup done by others. Immediate action includes: [15]

- Notifying the National Pollution Response Center by phoning 800-424-8802.
- Notifying the Coast Guard.
- Taking action to contain the spill, and contacting a spill response and cleanup company to assist, if necessary.

Be sure to give your insurance company the name and number of the Coast Guard representative you contacted.

Liability under OPA 90 creates a maritime lien against the vessel. The United States is authorized to take action against the vessel and the owner, or both.

Hazardous Materials (HAZMAT) Training.[16] All employees who are directly involved in hazardous materials transportation safety must be trained to prevent HAZMAT release. The list of HAZMAT materials runs for 162 pages, ranging from *accellerene* to *zinc peroxide*. Listed products commonly carried on boats are acetylene, batteries, caustic soda, freon, hydrochloric acid, propane, perforating guns, and paint. The penalty for violating the HAZMAT training requirement can be as high as $25,000 for each day of the violation. HAZMAT training is offered by major Coast Guard license preparation firms and other organizations. HAZMAT regulations are enforced by the Coast Guard.

Hazardous Waste Operations and Emergency Response (HAZWOPER) Training.[17] Employees designated to contain, control, and clean up spills involving hazardous materials must receive special training. HAZWOPER regulations are enforced by the Occupational Safety and Health Administration.

Dumping.[18] Under Annex V of the MARPOL treaty, it is illegal for any vessel to dump plastic trash anywhere in the oceans or the navigable waters of the United States. It is also illegal to dump the following items in the locations indicated:

- In lakes, rivers, bays, sounds, and up to 3 miles from shore: food, dunnage, rags, metal, lining and packing, glass, crockery, and materials that float.
- In waters from 3 to 12 miles from shore: dunnage, lining and packing, and materials that float. It is also illegal to dump the following unless ground smaller than one inch: food, rags, metal, glass, and crockery.
- In waters from 12 to 25 miles from shore: dunnage, lining and packing, and materials that float.

The restrictions of Annex V must be listed on placards or stickers placed at potential discharge sites on boats 26 feet or longer in length.

Marine Sanitation Devices. All vessels with an installed operable toilet must have an installed, certified marine sanitation device (MSD) attached to the toilet. Vessels 65 feet or shorter must install a Type I, II, or III MSD. Vessels longer than 65 feet must install a Type II or III MSD. Some inspected vessels shorter than 65 feet might have more stringent requirements.

Although federal law prohibits discharge of raw sewage from a vessel in U.S. territorial waters (within the 3-mile limit), states and other jurisdictions may have absolute no-discharge prohibitions on many waters.

ELIMINATING OR REDUCING RISK

You might decide not to insure against some risks, perhaps gambling that nothing unfavorable will happen. There is nothing wrong with such a decision, so long as you—and those dependent upon your business's income—are prepared for the consequences of loss. Here are some ways to reduce or eliminate risks that do not involve insurance:

Attorney Barry M. Snyder advises charter boat owners and captains to obey "The Golden Rule of Liability," by doing unto others as you would have them do unto you. Snyder explains that innumerable suits never would have been initiated if the charter operator had followed the Golden Rule. Charter operators must not only care for their customers, but also must let them know they care. They should be quick to say, "I don't think it was our fault, but let me accommodate you." The Golden Rule parallels the courts' insistence that a charter operator exercise "a very high degree of care." So keep the Golden Rule uppermost in mind and action, and make sure your employees do, too.

Find out whether your state has a Good Samaritan Act. [19] Such an act grants immunity from civil liability to a person who gratuitously and in good faith renders emergency care or treatment at the scene of an emergency away from a normal medical treatment site. The law generally dictates that the person being treated should have no objection, and the person treating should act as an ordinary, reasonably prudent person would act under similar circumstances.

You and any of your employees at the scene should be prepared to render assistance after an accident and to make required reports to authorities and your insurance carriers.

Be aware of the Limitation of Liability Act of 1851. [20] Under the act, an owner's liability in case of property damage or personal injury might be limited to the value of the vessel and its cargo. The key qualifying point of the act is whether the owner has "privity or knowledge" of what is happening. If not, the owner is not personally liable. The privity clause stems from the reason the act was conceived—to promote maritime investments by protecting shipowners who hired masters to load their vessels with cargo and deliver them to foreign ports. In case of damage or injuries outside of the owner's privity or knowledge, shipowners would be held liable for no more than their investment (vessel and cargo). The act can also apply to a bareboat charter party as owner. When setting up a charter operation, it is crucial to discuss with an attorney the possible applications of the Limitation of Liability Act.

If, as a licensed captain, you operate a charter vessel, you might eliminate the risk of your license being surrendered, deposited, suspended, or revoked (see chapter 13) by making sure your spouse or partner has a license—or by keeping a current list of dependable captains you could hire in an emergency.

Evaluate your business structure. Incorporation might provide needed protective insulation.

Know exactly what your insurance will cover in case of pollution. Establish an ongoing program for pollution prevention and for HAZMAT and HAZWOPER training. Don't spill and don't let your employees spill.

Be sure that each of your boats that is 26 feet in length or longer carries placards prohibiting illegal dumping. Placards can be obtained for a nominal charge from marinas, yards, ship's stores, and major Coast Guard license preparation firms.

Use the deck log to reduce risk. Ron Wahl, founder of Sea School, summarizes a classic case involving a 65-foot steel oysterboat. The owner had hired a captain to fish near a main channel off the mouth of the Mississippi River. For years, the captain anchored at night away from the channel, using required anchor lights.

> One night a small crew boat traveling at high speed left the channel and collided with the oysterboat. The crew boat was going so fast that it ran up on the bow of the oysterboat, slamming the crew boat captain's head through the windshield. In giving testimony, the

> captain said he then backed his boat off far enough to observe that the oysterboat had no anchor light. Even though there was evidence of an improperly used radar on the crew boat, the captain of the oysterboat had kept no log and could find no witness from the surrounding boats to verify that he was using an anchor light on that particular night. The court found the owner of the oysterboat liable for $140,000 in medical bills.

Says Wahl, "Even if the captain hadn't logged anything that night, it still would have been important to have kept a record showing that each previous night, at a particular time, somebody customarily turned on the light. It would have shown a systematic order of things that would indicate the light might also have been operating on the night of the collision."

Make radar an asset—not a liability. If your vessel is equipped with radar, and a collision occurs when the radar is not operating, the implication is that the collision might not have happened if the skipper had been using the radar. This would place the burden upon the skipper to prove that in failing to operate the radar, he or she was not negligent. If you have radar, use it any time another boat is near.

Establish a venue for litigation. If your charter operation is outside the continental United States, it might be prudent to include a clause in the charter agreement that the venue for claims against your company will be at your location. This can be effective in the case of a customer who decides to sue after returning home. The complaint would then have to be strong enough for the customer to choose to carry out the litigation where you operate. The clause also could protect you from the costs of transportation and lodging to reply to suits filed in the customer's hometown.

SELF-INSURING

You might also consider self-insurance, backed up with a contingency fund, in cases where the potential for loss is less than the cost of insurance. Let's say that you just paid $1,000 for an outboard motor and can buy theft insurance for $500 annually. However, you know that in an emergency you can buy a used motor for $700. You might decide to use a chain and padlock to secure the motor, set aside $500 this year for replacement, add a bit more next year, and forego theft insurance.

Another form of self-insurance is a deductible. For example, if the hull and machinery insurance on your $100,000 Offshore 33 has a deductible of 1 percent, you effectively have self-insured for the first thousand dollars of your vessel's value, in exchange for a reduced premium. Incidentally, you can shift that thousand dollars of risk to the customers just by requiring a $1,000 dollar security deposit.

SELECTING SHORESIDE INSURANCE

After eliminating or reducing some risks, and self-insuring against others, you eventually must transfer most of your remaining risks to an insurance carrier. In some cases your lender will require it.

The insurance you buy will cover risks encountered both ashore and afloat, and probably will be covered by more than one policy (e.g., life insurance, hazard insurance on a building, hull and machinery insurance on a vessel).

Property Loss

Determine the potential effect on the bottom line from loss or damage to each item you use in your business. You can then insure against such possible loss (along with taking protective measures). The following are examples:

- Fire and flood insurance for buildings and the property they contain. This type of insurance normally doesn't cover administrative records, cash, securities, or data contained on computer disks. Accordingly, your insurance plan should consider methods to protect them or back them up with extra copies. You also should determine whether any plate glass and glass display cases require separate coverage. You might decide to reduce glass-breakage risk by installing storm shutters or security shutters.
- Insurance for automobiles and other vehicles used in the business.
- Fidelity bonds. If you select this coverage for employees who handle large sums of money, an additional benefit will be the background information derived from the bonding process.
- Burglary and robbery insurance. This might be expanded for comprehensive hazards, such as counterfeit money and forged checks.

Loss of Business Income

Like a storm at sea, an income loss can occur when you least want it, but in either case you can be prepared. Give consideration to the following:

- Business interruption insurance. This can provide coverage for fixed expenses and expected profits during the time your business is closed due to circumstances beyond of your control.

- Personal insurance. Consider life and health insurance for you and your employees. Also decide upon key-person insurance for you, or to cover the death or disability of a partner or specially qualified employee.
- Liability insurance, and workers' compensation insurance. Straight liability insurance covers the safety of your employees and customers and malfunctions associated with your products and services. Workers' compensation insurance can protect you from extensive common-law obligations to your employees.

SELECTING MARINE INSURANCE

An *agent* is a person you deal with either face-to-face or over the telephone. [21] A *carrier* is the company that collects the premium, issues the policy, and pays the claim. A direct agent (or captive agent), such as an agent for State Farm or Allstate, deals with a single carrier. A managing agent, such as BOAT/U.S. and other boating organizations, represents a block of clients with a carrier, benefitting from discounts because of its volume of business. An independent agent is not tied to any carrier and sometimes can solve an insurance problem that a direct agent or managing agent cannot.

An independent agent who does not specialize in marine insurance may receive service from independent intermediaries or wholesalers. What this means to you is that the agent who handles your shoreside insurance might be able to arrange your marine insurance through a wholesaler.

No matter whom you deal with, when it's time to file a claim, you will want the carrier to be in business and to fulfill that part of the policy agreement with a smile and a check. You can select from some three hundred underwriters that offer marine insurance. Search through the trade magazines for your type of charter operation, and also try the Yellow Pages. Talk with other charter operators. Select carriers with the kind of track record you can be comfortable with and compare their rates.

Also contact associations that serve as managing agents for group insurance programs. These associations can spread underwriting risks by insulating the underwriter from regional catastrophes. For example, the National Association of Charterboat Operators (NACO) manages a group insurance program that even pays the costs of a marine survey for policyholders who have been insured with the program for more than one year.[22] Also, dive-boat and dive-shop operators can generally count on the certifying agencies for insurance availability. And the American Water Ski Association offers insurance for its members.

Your insurance plan will evaluate the following types of marine insurance:

1. Insurance for the boat, generally called hull and machinery insurance.
2. Insurance for cargo carried for hire.
3. Liability insurance, called protection and indemnity (P&I).
4. Miscellaneous personal property insurance.
5. License insurance.

Marine Hull and Machinery Insurance

Actual cash value versus agreed value. Insuring your hull and machinery for "actual cash value" might provide a bargain-rate premium, but it could be a major mistake in your insurance plan. An *actual-cash-value* settlement covers only the depreciated value of the boat and its accessories, and the policy might authorize the *carrier* to determine the depreciated value.

An actual-cash-value policy poses no problem if your insurance plan allows for it. Otherwise you should insure for an agreed value, which is the amount you would expect to pay to buy another boat and continue your charter operation.

The carrier. Before insuring a boat, a carrier's representative wants to know everything about it: age, construction materials, condition, electronics, navigational systems, fire-fighting systems, engine, type of fuel, where it is operated and by whom, and so on. This information comes from a marine surveyor, who normally is hired by the owner.

The surveyor. The surveyor should go over the boat in the water as well as out, and should inspect and try *everything*. That includes engine, through-hulls, seacocks, plumbing, electrical, electronics, ground tackle, rigging, lifelines, hull, shaft, prop, cutlass bearing, rudder, operating systems—*everything*.

The surveyor's report should list major problems as well as minor ones. Normally, if the owner shows proof that the major problems have been corrected, the underwriter will insure the boat, provided that:

- The operator or operators are satisfactory, e.g., licensed captains, with appropriate experience for the boat.
- The boat will be used for the purposes for which insured, and is documented and inspected accordingly, if required (see chapters 8 and 10).
- The boat will be operated in waters for which it is insured.

Bear in mind that, if you are a prospective buyer, you can use a survey report as a negotiating instrument. When you receive the report, you can ask the seller to resolve the major problems—and even the minor ones—as a condition of sale. Then, if you consummate the sale, you can use the survey report to obtain your insurance (see appendix A).

Marine Insurance for Cargo Carried for Hire

Cargo insurance is available to the charter operator/owner, the shipper, the receiver, and the consignee. An operator/owner who customarily carries cargo might want an "open policy," whereas an operator who normally carries only passengers might consider single-occasion cargo insurance when necessary.

Marine Liability Insurance—Protection and Indemnity (P&I)

P&I generally covers liabilities resulting from the operation of the boat, except physical damages to the vessel itself, damage to other property you own, and losses payable under the hull policy.

Marine Miscellaneous Personal Property Insurance

This coverage is generally an add-on option to commercial marine insurance.

Marine License Insurance

License insurance can provide paid legal representation in case of marine casualties and paid legal defense against license actions, civil penalty actions, and civil lawsuits. It also can replace income lost due to license suspension or revocation and can provide coverage for civil judgments, fines, and penalties. Companies that specialize in license insurance advertise in professional maritime publications and in the Yellow Pages of major port cities. Also check maritime associations and maritime unions.

PREPARE AND REVIEW YOUR INSURANCE PLAN

Your insurance plan becomes a section in your business plan. To be sure you overlook nothing, you might use this chapter as a checklist and list every possible risk to your charter operation. Include real estate, vehicles, office equipment, appliances, employees, customers, your life and health and that of your key assistants, the boat, personal property carried aboard, marine cargo, your captain's license, your dock, pollution, and anything else the loss of which might cause serious risk to your business.

Now, annotate how you will handle each risk (reduce it, accept it, self-insure, or insure). For risks you don't insure, explain how you will reduce them, or why you will accept them. For risks you insure, add the company, type of insurance, premium, and effective dates.

Schedule periodic insurance reviews, and be prepared for unscheduled reviews, such as upon the advent of civil unrest or approaching hazardous weather. During each review seek out potential casualties and incipient liabilities, and translate your discoveries into corrective measures.

Here are examples: If Captain Hotshot keeps ignoring preventive maintenance, perhaps you should hire another captain before you find you need another boat. If all hands aren't treating your hazardous materials properly, institute a system whereby they will. If your dive boats are taking customers out when the weather forecast says they shouldn't, reevaluate your income projection. If customers are not being treated according to the Golden Rule of Liability, make sure they are.

Verify that your policy's hull and machinery value is in line with the current market value of the boat. Confirm that the navigational limitations on the policy specifically include the areas where you actually operate your boat. Check that the policy accurately reflects how your boat is stored during any lay-up periods. And, to ensure continuing coverage, make sure that warranties you made when you purchased the policy, for example, that you would keep it equipped with radar, are still valid. [23]

SUMMARY

1. An insurance plan evaluates how to manage the risks of property loss, loss of business income, and liability.
2. A charter operator can manage risks in three ways: (1) eliminate or reduce them; (2) transfer them to an insurer; and/or (3) accept them.
3. Maritime legal actions can be taken against an owner, a skipper, a skipper's license, the boat involved, or all four.
4. A boat with a maritime lien can be seized. If the owner does not execute a bond or a letter of undertaking, the boat might be sold.
5. A boat can be seized on the spot for a contraband violation.
6. Don't spill. If you do, be prepared to pay for the cleanup.
7. A charter operator wants to be sure the insurer will stay in business and will pay claims, regardless of premium costs.
8. Group insurance rates can be less expensive than one-to-one insurance.
9. The deck log can be worth a six-figure insurance policy.
10. Use radar if you have it.
11. Make a written insurance plan and review it often.

CHAPTER 4

Marketing Tools

The marketing section of most major bookstores contains shelves of books on advertising, direct-mail marketing, and public relations. Attempting to squeeze that information into a single chapter of this book would be like trying to compress Chapman, Dutton, Bowditch, and the Nautical Almanac into a single pamphlet. However, I have summarized basic concepts as stepping stones for newcomers and reminders for others. These concepts were gleaned from the marketing and sales books listed in the notes.[1] My study and use of those books has led me to embrace two marketing principles that have always worked:

1. Most marketers and salespersons know that the old fashioned hard sell just doesn't work, because you can't "sell" something to a person who doesn't want it. In the chartering business, you can get a prospect to spend discretionary income only by offering something he or she wants or needs. Find out what that is, package it so that the prospect will perceive it to fill that want or need, price it right, get the prospect to inspect the package, and you have a sale.
2. The customer must perceive that your charter operation provides something special that no competitor offers. This *differentiation* comes from the way you *position* the company through marketing. It involves a marketing technique variously known as a "single most important tactic," a "unique selling proposition," or simply "a competitive advantage." Differentiation creates something you want the customer to remember when thinking of your business. It should put your company in a position in the marketplace that your competitor will have difficulty copying. And it should be adaptable to a slogan or motto. Examples:

"We try harder"; "Don't leave home without it"; "You're in good hands with . . ."; "Everyday low prices."

There might be other ways to make sales, but these two are proven. They are referred to throughout the chapter and throughout the book.

YOUR DATABASE

This book refers to a prime marketing tool called a *database*. For our purposes, a database is a file, or several files, of customers, contacts, prospects, and media addressees (for public relations). In a rudimentary form, it is nothing more than a handful of scribbled scraps of paper containing a few names and phone numbers. In a more efficient format, it is a computerized file containing everything you need in order to maintain a customer profile, launch advertising promotions, carry out direct-mail marketing, conduct public relations, and measure marketing promotions. "Database" in this book refers to the computerized version, although it does not exclude a well-organized manual database.

To build a customer profile, your database should include standard identifying information, plus data about age, sex, occupation, income, education, marital status, number and age of children, membership in organizations, special interests, media used, and more. Why? Because when you prospect for additional customers, you will want to search for people similar to the ones you have.

An inexpensive internal method of collecting database information requires only a pad of forms and a pencil. Ask your customers and drop-ins to fill out a form, "so we can put you on our mailing list." Also collect information from telephone contacts, letters, charter application forms, and responses to sales promotions. And don't forget secondary sources, such as the Yellow Pages, and criss-cross directories (also called city directories) in the library that cross-reference names, addresses, phone numbers, and occupations.

HOW TO PREPARE AN AD FOR ANY MEDIUM

Successful charter operators don't labor to make their ads "cute," or to copy Madison Avenue; they strive for the bottom line. They measure each ad's effectiveness mathematically, such as by using return-on-promotion (ROP) formulas. ROP shows how many queries you received per dollar spent on an ad, how many sales you made, and the percentage you earned upon your promotional costs. The figures produced allow you to compare numerous promotional results with the same yardstick. Find an ad with the best ROP analysis and stick with it until you develop one better (see appendix F for return on promotion and break-even analysis).

As an aid to measurement, the messages in your ads should remain in focus, even though the method of delivery will vary with the medium you select. For instance, if your boat is positioned as the only Coast Guard-certified charter vessel in the harbor, every ad should hit that point.

Charter operators who study ads find that they fit into a group of standard formulas. An example that you can modify for use in any ad is the classic AIDA formula: Attention, Interest, Desire, Action.

First analyze your unique selling proposition and focus on the special something that you will promise the prospect. Now:

Attract ATTENTION, with a striking headline or lead that promises the benefits the customer simply must have—money, health, love, sex, self-esteem, escape.

Develop INTEREST, to show why a purchase will provide those benefits. Use proven words that produce results, like *free*, *you*, *results*, *save*, *sale*, *guarantee*, *proven*, *money*, *discover*, *health*, *easy*, *safety*, *now*, *new*, and *love*.

Stimulate DESIRE to take advantage of this offer *now*—end of season, imminent price increase, limited staterooms.

Call for ACTION. Show how the prospect can respond (telephone number, coupon), and why he or she must do so to have the promise made come true! And be sure the ad itself fulfills the promise it made at the beginning.

You can use variations of the AIDA formula in all forms of advertising described in the following sections.

ADVERTISING

The following advertising tools are described in this section: advertising specialties; brochures and fliers; bulletin boards; business cards and stationery; catalogs; charter brokers; cross-promotions; demonstrations; exhibiting at boat shows and other trade shows; outdoor advertising, personal letters; phone cards; point-of-purchase ads; postcards; print media ads; radio; samples; seminars; television; window displays; and Yellow Pages.

Advertising Specialties

Advertising specialties are relatively inexpensive items, such as pens, pencils, license plates and frames, bumper stickers, glassware, calendars, matches, key chains, napkins, ball caps, T-shirts, searchlights, balloons, tethered balloons, pennants, banners, decals, badges, or anything else that works. A prospect with one of your specialties has your company name, phone number, and slogan within easy reach.

Look up "Advertising Specialties" in the Yellow Pages for businesses that provide these items.

Brochures and Fliers

A brochure is a multipage marketing tool, whereas a flier (also called a circular) is generally a single sheet or a foldover. Each can be used as a stand-alone piece or as part of a package. Each should be created to fit into its position in your selling process, such as:

- To answer inquiries.
- As point-of-purchase literature.
- As part of a direct-mail marketing package.
- For use during sales presentations.
- As a press kit insertion.
- As leave-behind literature.
- For boat show and other trade show distribution.

Because of their lesser costs, fliers are excellent for large-volume handouts at boat shows, on countertops in hotel and motel lobbies, under windshield wipers, during door-to-door distribution, at visitor welcome centers, and for general correspondence.

Use brochures for interested prospects. Try offering a free brochure through a small ad. Under this two-step form of advertising, every return you get should be from an interested customer, worth the cost of the ad and the brochure. Mail the brochure and place the customer information into your database for followup.

Brochures and fliers can be printed at lower cost if ordered in quantity, making the total cost less than that for a large newspaper or magazine ad. Copy and artwork represent a one-time investment and may be cost-free if already bought as part of an ad. Spreading the cost over a period of time makes brochures and fliers even more inexpensive.

The following pointers will help you prepare a brochure or flier:

- Plan a written and visual sales message for the cover that will grab the reader.
- Write the brochure for a specific reader.
- Arrange it in short sections, in logical order.
- Use striking subheads that will encourage the prospect to read more, but will tell the story when standing alone.
- Include visuals that make your product real and that emphasize the key selling points.
- Be sure the brochure answers every question that the reader might ask at that point in the sales process.

- Make the prospect want to keep it, perhaps by including a calendar, discount coupon, or advertising specialty.
- Be sure it contains everything the prospect needs to know about ordering, payment, and guarantees.
- End with a call for action.

Bulletin Boards

Consider using these no-cost media for special signs, business cards, fliers, or even brochures. Bulletin boards at marinas, bait shops, and ship's stores can be ideal spots. Along the waterfront, or in other targeted market areas, try restaurants, supermarkets, coin laundries, sporting-goods stores, hotels, and motels. Post enough copies so that each interested prospect can take one.

Business Cards and Stationery

A business card needs your name, address, phone number, logo, and a reminder of your unique selling proposition. The reverse side will be an added asset if it carries advertising copy or printed information that will influence a person to keep it. What about a review of Federal Communications Commission regulations for VHF radio, or a listing of the fishing bag limits, or a guaranteed charter discount upon return of the card?

Business cards and every item of stationery should carry the company image—logo and motto. They should be printed on stock befitting the image you want for your charter operation.

Catalogs

If you are going to sell a large number of products, such as through a ship's store, you might opt to expand your operation into a full-fledged mail-order business. If so, remember that a catalog is a store away from your store, and reflects your company image.

As a store, the catalog becomes a showroom that should grab your customers and lead them to what they need or want to buy. To help the customers, organize each page logically, using a repeated layout format so that they get used to the same gaze motion (eye movement) on each page.

Put your best-sellers and products with the highest markup on the inside front cover, inside back cover, and outside back cover. Position a letter from the owner near the front, and place a prominent, accessible table of contents on the first right-hand page. If the catalog is small, reserve the centerfold for your most important promotion. Include ordering information on each page.

Make each headline a head jerker, and treat each item as a separate, complete ad. Answer every question concerning a product a prospect might have. If a single question remains unanswered, the prospect won't buy.

The order form should be a separate, easy-to-fill-out blank, on smaller, heavier stock than the other pages, bound into the catalog. Be sure it makes ordering easy, with the coupon, shipping cost, 800 number, fax number, and credit card information easy to understand and use. Include a prominent guarantee, and don't forget a business reply envelope.

Charter Brokers

Many a charter operator lets a charter broker do the bulk of the marketing. The owner generally insures and maintains the boat and agrees to the charter fee; the broker does the advertising, mails out information, checks customer references, and executes the contracts. See the introduction for more on charter brokers and charter companies.

Cross-Promotions

A cross-promotion can merge marketing campaigns of two noncompeting organizations for the good of both. For instance, it can use one company's fliers in a second company's mailout of bills. With a specialized mailing list, it can give a charter operator better control than through newspaper or electronic media advertising. And it can facilitate discounting prices without losing credibility.

Here's an example of maintaining price credibility. Captain Fishmaster advertises his head boat for $45 per person per day, but would like to obtain additional customers by discounting. If he advertises a discounted price every other week at $35, his $45 price loses credibility. Why would anybody willingly pay $45 if they know that Fishmaster can make a decent profit at $35? So Fishmaster makes an agreement with a nearby beach motel. He prepares fliers for the motel, offering its guests a day of fishing for $10 off the regular price of $45—compliments of the hotel. The hotel gets free promotion and Captain Fishmaster gets his discount without losing price credibility.

Demonstrations

The cost of a demonstration is nothing more than the cost of using the site. Use demonstrations as tools for immediate sales. Run a demonstration of four or five minutes, and follow it with a closing (sales or order taking). I once saw a dive-boat operator running underwater demonstrations in his scuba gear, and surfacing to sign up students at "boat show prices." (Trade-show discounts seldom cause a price credibility crisis.) At another time I saw a fishing guide selling his own manufactured lures, three at a time, by casting into a 40-foot tank containing bass and catching them, over and over.

Exhibiting at Boat Shows and Other Trade Shows

Schoolchildren often have a "show and tell" day. A charter operator who uses a boat show for a "show and tell" day is making no money. It should be a "show and sell" day. Although institutional marketing and database development are factors, the money and time a boat show takes means that you should show *and* sell.

Distribute brochures and fliers, run a video showing how easy and how much fun it is to charter with Double Anchor Chartering—but *sell*. Offer charter reservations at "boat-show discounts" for customers who leave a deposit.

Keep the credit-card imprinter and reservation receipt book ready. Be sure each person operating the booth knows how to use them. And always sponsor a sign-up for a prize, in order to add to the database.

The exhibit has to be the best you can create, or afford to have produced. A prospect judges your entire operation by the only example available—your exhibit, whether it be hand-lettered or professionally crafted, smudgy or spotless, jury-rigged or top-of-the-line, questionable or trustworthy.

Imagine what the competition will use; then decide whether to build your own exhibit in the garage or to purchase a professional one. Unless you are exceptionally qualified in garage work, find "Display Designers and Producers" in the Yellow Pages, and arrange to visit one of their warehouses for ideas. Perhaps you can rent an exhibit setup from them, or you may want them to construct one. Consider sharing the cost with an exhibitor whose products are compatible with your chartering business.

Outdoor Ads

Outdoor advertising media include signs; billboards; bus and taxi signs; painted walls and roofs; banners; posters; signs on your vehicles; and names, signs, or pennants on your boats.

Like all other visual advertising, outdoor ads must be placed where the target customers can read them. For instance, in a destination resort area, a charter company's sign on a bus serving a lower-income peripheral district probably would provide a terrible ROP (return on promotion); the same sign on a tram operating a loop in the exclusive center of the resort might bring in a good one.

In the charter business, much outdoor advertising is indirect or institutional advertising. It can, however, provide sales in the right situation. For example, a billboard that reads "Cold pop and beer next right" might produce a good ROP. So might a billboard at the edge of a fishing village announcing "Bill's Bait & Boat Shop—At the Bridge."

When preparing the ad for a billboard, remember that most passing motorists will have time to read only about six words. So a billboard should:

- Deliver the message in five seconds.
- Deliver the selling promise in words and pictures.
- Identify your charter operation at a glance.
- Avoid abstract and symbolic artwork and photographs.
- Contain pure, bright colors on a white background.
- Use no more than three elements in the design.
- Use an easy-to-remember phone number. A twenty-four-hour telemarketer, 800-FLOWERS, drew two thousand responses the first week.

Personal Letters

Personal letters are inexpensive and particularly suited to small businesses. A personal letter must not look like the computer-personalized form letters used for direct-mail ads. It should appeal to the addressee's interests by including personal information that you have gleaned from the database, from your own observation, from the chamber of commerce, or from any other source. It can end with a demand for action (*call me, stop by to talk, mail back the enclosed form with date available*), or with a statement that you will be following up in the near future.

Phone Cards

Phone cards, used for more than a decade in Europe, have become a viable advertising tool in the United States. You can purchase cards for a certain number of either minutes or dollars of long-distance use. The card's account balance is kept in a magnetic strip or is tapped through a touch-tone 800 number. Don't forget company name, phone, logo, and motto on each card.

Point-of-Purchase Ads

A customer comes in to charter a houseboat on Lunker Lake and sees a sign: "The Complete Fishing Guide to Lunker Lake—On Sale Here—$3.50." On the sign are scattered pictures of bass, catfish, and crappie; it says that the book explains catch limits, how to catch, how to clean, how to cook, and everything else a charterer needs to know if he's brand-new to Lunker Lake. Or a customer returns from a week's sailboat charter and, upon checking in with the charter operator, sees a sign: "Discounts now for charters next season." In each case, the prospective customers have already proven they are willing to pay for similar products or services, which are *right there in the store*.

Many manufacturers and distributors will provide point-of-purchase ads free if the ads will help sell their products. The ads might include anything from a small countertop board declaring "Authorized distributor of Acme dive equipment," to an electrically lighted sign advertising a soft drink. Operating without them is like operating a bait shop with tanks for goldfish and minnows, and leaving the tank empty.

Postcards

Postcards work well as announcements, invitations, discount coupons, and order forms. Consider using them in lieu of letters when possible, because they are more likely to be read, and postage is less expensive. A flashy or fluorescent color will attract attention and sometimes will produce extra returns.

Print Media Ads

Print media ads can be display, classified, or classified display ads. A classified or classified display ad functions something like the Yellow Pages; people looking for *your* type of operation will find your ad. A straight display ad, on the other hand, demands originality and proper location in order to attract attention.

A city newspaper can reach 80 to 90 percent of all families living in the city. But if, say, 97 percent of the readers think of water only as something to drink, the cost of advertising would have to be very low to give you a decent ROP. A beach newspaper, however, might be another story. And a magazine published for the waterfront might hit big time. You can determine the best publication and best ad only by running test ads and measuring the results, one variable at a time.

When testing, try placing the same ad in several publications, perhaps offering a free brochure, with a different "department" in your return address for each publication, and measure results. Another method is to offer a different discount or other "special" in competing publications. A minor word change sometimes can make a nonproducing ad productive, so try changing ads slightly in the same publication and measure those results. Again, test only one variable at a time.

You will want to advertise in publications where your competition routinely advertises, for two reasons. First, people are used to seeing charter advertisements in those publications and will look for them when they decide to charter.

And second, the competitor must be getting sufficient business from them to continue to advertise.

Radio

Each radio station has a format—rock, country music, background music, talk, news, etc. You will want your ads to be played by stations that use the format your customers like. And you will want your ads to be played when your customers are listening.

Although your research might give you an idea of customer likes and listening times, you still have to test. You might advertise with three or four stations, offering a different discount on each. For example, on one station, a dive-boat operator offers free air fills for six weeks for Sunday dive-trip customers; on another station the same operator offers a spare-parts kit; on another, a set of dive tables. The operator then would measure the response to each offer and add or cancel stations according to the results.

Listeners constantly change stations and are used to ignoring commercials, often driving with only half an ear tuned to the radio. To reach them, your ads should be played over and over. Here are guidelines for an effective radio ad:

- It must convert visuals into words and sound-pictures.
- It cannot be subtle. For example, if you are seeking requests for a brochure, make this clear over and over. How many ads have you heard, then asked yourself, "What did they want?"
- It should include urgency, such as a time limit or the date a sale ends. Otherwise, even an interested prospect will say, "I want to charter one of their boats someday," and will return to whatever he or she was doing before hearing the ad.
- It should include a phone number for response, repeated twice.
- It should end with the phone number, and with nothing following the number—especially not a witty remark. You want your customer to remember your phone number, not a cute joke.
- The ad will work right away or not at all. Don't stay with a loser.
- If it is successful, repeat it. Listeners who push buttons may never hear a one-time spot.
- A thirty-second spot will accomplish almost as much as a sixty-second one. Give your ROP some cost-effective leverage.

Samples

Minimal-cost sampling can develop intense customer interest, coupled with a feeling of loyalty to the operator who provided the sample. A sailing-school operator or dive-shop operator with a top-notch operation could offer a sample class. A charter powerboat operator might take prospects once around the bay and let them steer. A fish camp operator or a houseboat charter operator might pass out samples of smoked fish caught in the river or lake.

Seminars

For a seminar, think in terms of a forty-five-minute lecture, ending with a sales closing. I attended a seminar prepared by a charter operator who offered reduced charter rates for members of his cruising club. The seminar was given by a captain who exuded cruising camaraderie like a politician exudes good times. After explaining the advantages of club membership, he played a video of a recent cruise, showing happy sailors who happened to be wearing club patches. At the conclusion of the seminar, he obtained four family memberships from the eight couples attending, and two of the new members signed up for the next cruise. Money from both directions. Marvelous!

The seminar was given on the dock, but it could have taken place at a motel or hotel. The operator might have advertised, but he didn't need to, because the sports editor of the local paper and a local radio announcer both ran his news release offering a free seminar on how to cruise. In addition, he had written a few personal letters and had made some telephone calls. The seminar was exceptional because the participants were a select market of people who *knew* they would like to cruise even before they arrived at the seminar.

Television

A television ad has to catch the viewer in the first few seconds or it will fail. The ad must be *visual*, supported by voice, music, and sound. A sailing-school ad, for instance, might present a boat under full sail in a warm, fresh wind, with the water singing under the hull, then cut to confident, healthy-looking people on-board casually handling lines. The announcer's audio meanwhile would be implying, "See how easy it is. This could by *you*." The ad would close with visual and audio repeating the company name and phone number, or address.

The cost of television advertising depends upon the time at which it is aired (which equates to the number of people watching). Most charter operators would not consider prime time—from eight to eleven P.M.—because of the expense. Few would consider fringe time, which is before and after prime time. Although costs for time after midnight become tiny, so does the audience. And if your customer profile is male, you probably would steer clear of daytime television, because of the preponderance of women viewers.

But there are ways to advertise effectively to a television audience at less than prime or fringe-time cost. For example, a local TV station (either broadcast or cable) might cost less than a major affiliate, while reaching the same market. Also, ads played after midnight can reach people with videocassette recorders who tape special programs and view them later.

Commercial fishermen will watch early morning weather programs and fishing reports before heading out each day. Sportfishermen will crowd the airwaves for the same reasons on early Saturday mornings.

In addition, do not neglect local TV channels that provide bulletin-board service. Productive ads on some of these channels contain little more than a couple of lines of print—over and over, all day long!

Although you can pay a television station or a local producer to prepare your commercial, you might want to create the concept first. Here are formats that work:

- Demonstrate the product in action, to emphasize a benefit or benefits.
- Compare the product with other comparable products.
- Use a testimonial from a customer, for credibility, or to exploit sincere emotion.
- Have a stand-up presenter fire a powerful, straightforward sales pitch.
- Show how the product fits into users' life-styles.
- Show a slice-of-life scene involving the product.
- Use a jingle that will imprint itself on the viewer's mind.
- Create a fictional character, such as the Jolly Green Giant.
- Provide reasons why people use the product.
- Try humor, but be wary of its being misinterpreted.
- Use cartoons for children, such as in an ad showing why children should wear your specially designed life jackets.

If you hire a TV station to prepare the ad, here is a list of questions to help you ensure that the ad has a good chance for success:

- Does it exploit a single, most important tactic (unique selling proposition) visually—with words, music, and sound added to clarify and strengthen the visual?
- When viewed with no sound, does it deliver its message with pictures only?
- Does it catch the viewer in the first few seconds?
- Does it give your message at the beginning, present it in different words in the middle, and summarize it at the end?
- Does it show your product in action and name it whenever possible?
- With only thirty, sixty, or a hundred and twenty seconds to sell, does it sell every second?

- Is it limited to a thirty-second spot, or perhaps sixty seconds, except for direct response (e.g., asking for a telephone reply) which does well with two minutes?
- Does it warn viewers early if they will need to jot down an address or phone number?
- Does it give the address and directions to your boat or showroom?
- Does it introduce the celebrity, if one is used?
- Does it avoid overloading the viewer with complex visuals, coupled with a fusillade of words, by going heavy on one and light on the other?
- Is the ad too overwhelming for your product? (Sell the charter, not the commercial.)

Window Displays

A storefront or office window that contains only your company name is like a bag of money buried in the front yard. It's not going to earn a penny. Yacht charter services can display color photographs of their boats, along with special rate offerings; fishing boat operators can display boats, motors, fishing tackle, photographs of prize-winners, and mounted trophies; dive shops can present special offerings of merchandise and services.

Yellow Page Ads

Why should you list in the Yellow Pages? Because people looking in the Yellow Pages are ready to buy. If your listing is not there and a competitor's is, you have just lost a sale, and possibly a long-term customer.

Must you have a display ad as well as a listing? Probably, if your competition has one. And make your ad as big as your competitor's, even though he or she might have four times the number of boats you operate. An equal-sized ad makes the customer perceive both of you as equals. And if your ad is more focused on the selling proposition that only you offer, you have the edge.

Hit the readers with your single most important tactic and add the attributes of your business. Let customers know why they should call you instead of the competition. Do you accept credit cards? Do you have a toll-free number for long-distance customers? Do you have a twenty-year safety record or an unequaled guarantee? Tell them. And measure the results through customer interviews.

Your measurements might reveal that you should list in more than one category (fishing/bait shops, dive charters/diving certification), or in additional directories (local, adjoining communities, customer target areas in other states).

And keep this in mind about the Yellow Pages: any time you *tell* somebody you are in the Yellow Pages, you are steering them to the ads of your direct competition. Tell them, "You'll find us in the white pages."

DIRECT-MAIL MARKETING

Direct-mail marketing provides an advanced tool in today's multisegmented marketplace by harnessing the computer to track prospects and customers. Direct mail provides the means to measure results of every step of your promotion—your offer, its packaging, your mailing list, and the response rate. Although direct marketing can be completed in one step—where the prospect responds by chartering—it can also be used as a two-step operation. The first step adds to the database, and the second exploits that addition. Let's consider an ideal one-step promotion.

Ideally, if you wanted to sell fifty contracts on your Icewater Charters expedition, you would send a direct-mail package to fifty people who need or want a cold-weather charter trip. Each recipient would be irresistibly compelled to open the package and would respond to the offer by placing an immediate order.

In the real world, we create a package containing an offer, send it to a targeted list of prospects whom we believe will respond, measure the results and refine the packaging, the offer, and the mailing list in order to increase the response rate. The list and all three parts of the package must be measured: the envelope, the contents, and the means to reply (see appendix F for measuring return on promotion and break-even analysis.)

The List

Depending upon your marketing plan, you can extract a mailing list from your database or rent a list (on computer disk, tape, CD-ROM, or preprinted labels) from a list broker or owner. When renting a list, your customer profile comes into play, because you want the prospects on the list to fit that profile as closely as possible.

You also might have the option to exchange lists with another company, or even work out a package insert in a noncompetitor's mailing. And you might consider taking advantage of a co-op mailing, by having your promotion inserted in a "card deck" of postage-paid postcards. (Your card should be on or near the top of a card deck to ensure that the recipient reads it before losing interest.)

The Envelope

The goal is to get the prospect to *open* the envelope. Test self-mailers versus letter packages; personalized versus nonpersonalized approaches; number 10 envelopes versus 6-by-9s or jumbos; teaser approaches versus blind envelopes; stamps versus bulk metered mail; first-class mail versus third class; and mailing labels versus direct-print addresses. Try plain white envelopes that look like personal mail, unusual envelopes, or unusual statements on the envelopes.

The Contents

The letter must gain the reader's attention in five seconds, or it will be discarded. It should be a personalized, one-on-one version of a combination letter, written ad, and brochure, selling a single, fantastic, you-must-have product or service. The offer must be compelling and must end with a call to action *now*, or the recipient will toss it away.

Other items in the package should promote the offer. These might be an advertising specialty, a brochure or flier, a photograph of your yacht, a catalog, a reprint of favorable publicity, a videotape, a testimonial, or anything else that might work.

The Means to Reply

Include a card, envelope, toll-free number, order form, or an involvement device (like a sticker to place on a square). The means to reply must be easy for the prospect to find and simple to use. A return-mail device should be self-addressed with postage paid.

PUBLIC RELATIONS

In advertising you *pay* someone to inform your prospects that they should try your charter service. In public relations you *influence* somebody to try it, or to inform prospects that they should try it. If your PR campaign succeeds, you have essentially created free advertising.

Imagine paying $6,000 or more for a full-page ad. And imagine paying only the cost of postage and stationery for a news release that runs a full page—in boating publications all over the country. That's the excitement of public relations!

Public relations is institutional advertising that engenders legitimacy and credibility because it is not paid advertising. Like all institutional advertising, it can generate direct and indirect sales. This can produce immediate revenue while establishing name recognition and brand acceptance for the long haul.

The two top public relations techniques are good will and credible newsworthiness. Forge them into one and you have an unbeatable tool.

Goodwill

In chapter three I mentioned attorney and licensed captain Barry Snyder's Golden Rule of Liability: Do unto others as you would have them do unto you. Snyder explains that it's more than just a rule. It is an outgoing positive attitude of care toward your business and your customers. If you have it, it sparkles like sunshine over your entire operation. It's goodwill and it sells. Here's an example:

When doing research for this book, I discovered two charter operators I thought would be interesting to mention in the book. I decided to call both and, as I usually do, identify myself and my quest and ask for a convenient time I might call back.

The individual who answered the first number replied, "Uh, the president doesn't speak for publication over the telephone to people he doesn't know. If you write a letter and describe what you're looking for, maybe he'll answer." (Unfortunately, I'm not making this up.)

Calling the second business, I was transferred to a busy president, who nevertheless ordered her calls held and spent twenty minutes with me. Her excitement and knowledge about her niche and the industry was so infectious that I decided I would buy her products and services any time. Of course, I never wrote to the first charter operator, because his spokesman hadn't offered me an ounce of goodwill. And you don't have to guess which company made its way into the book.

Newsworthiness

How do you become newsworthy if you do nothing except rent boats and perform maintenance? Generate your own news. Here is what four charter operators do:

- A fishing guide with a boat and tackle store sponsors an annual fishing contest. He gets publicity, sells bait, tackle, and boats, and sometimes wins his own contest!
- A charter company operator sponsors an annual race, along with a special division for boats she charters at discount prices.
- After a burglar steals a prized tropical fish collection from a home in Florida, a dive-shop operator takes a group of graduates into the Gulf of Mexico and nets replacements.
- A sailing-school operator cosponsors a community softball league, offering a free sail for the winning team.

When you generate a newsworthy item, tell the media about it through news releases (also called press releases or publicity releases), which you create and deliver (see section on news releases). And tell your customers and prospects about it (see section on newsletters).

The following checklist offers ideas for generating your own news:

- Develop or introduce a new product or service.
- Upgrade your vessel or equipment.
- Find a new or unusual use for your boat.
- Announce a new captain or an upgraded Coast Guard license.
- Publish a new brochure or catalog.

- Gain a client who is well-known or controversial.
- Start or plan a joint venture.
- Become an officer in an organization.
- Participate in a community enterprise or a charitable activity.
- Publish an annual report.
- Tie your operation in with the news of the day. Schedule your excursion boat to meet a warship returning from (or commencing) a deployment. Offer TV coverage of breaking news or a sheduled event aboard your fishing vessel at sea.
- Reorganize.
- Release useful information to put your business into your readers' minds.
- Form a committee to protect your industry, or make it safer or better for your customers.
- Sponsor an award or a scholarship.
- Make a newsworthy prediction about the weather, the industry, or any other subject involving your charter operation that will get attention and promote sales without your losing credibility.
- Celebrate your business anniversary.
- Make a state-of-the-industry release.
- Publish a celebrity testimonial.
- Write a profile, a guest article, a question-and-answer article, a how-to article, or a case history for a local newspaper or boating publication, or any other document that your prospective customers read.
- Start a column, or have a columnist mention your business.
- Get on a radio or television talk show.
- Stage an event or do something incredible, like holding a "fishathon" for kids or a "pirate invasion" for grown kids.
- Give a speech, a fishing seminar, or a boating safety lecture.
- Organize or sponsor a parade.
- Throw a party.
- Open a new ship's store or a new branch.
- Hold an open house or a guided tour of the vessel, or give a grand opening.
- Become known as an expert on something related to your business.

News Releases

A news release is a typed or computer-printed, double-spaced factual report explaining who, what, where, when, why, and how something newsworthy happened. For print media, accompanying photography helps increase chances for publication, if it's the type that the publication can routinely process (5 × 7 black and white print or larger, sometimes color slide or color prints—check with the publication).

To ensure that the release goes to the right person, call the newspaper, radio station, or television station and get that person's name. At a large newspaper, your release might be best suited for the sports editor, the outdoors editor, the fishing editor, or the boating editor. (On a small paper, one person might handle all of those jobs.) If your release is big news, the news editor or the city editor might want to see it. Radio and television stations have similar job descriptions—often called sports director, and so forth, all the way up to coanchor and anchor. In most cases, you should identify the person by name and title.

There is no way in the world that you can be guaranteed that your release will be run. But it has a good chance if it indeed contains *news*. Buying a new charter boat might not be news, but buying one specially designed for local whale watching might be.

As you continue to issue legitimate news releases, you should cultivate your contacts for best leverage. For example, work harder with an editor who has a circulation of fifty-thousand than you would with an editor who has a circulation of ten thousand. But be aware that ten editors with a circulation of one thousand each might run any reasonably written release you send, whereas one editor with a larger circulation might expect more than ten times the effort. Further, as you continue to explore the system, you will want to consider which publications will actually be read by your targeted customers.

The heading. The release can be on company letterhead. Identify it at the top of the first page as "News Release" (or "Press Release"). On the next line, place the words "For Immediate Release." On the following line, insert the preparation date, then the words, "For Further Information," along with the name and phone number of a knowledgeable contact person in your company. Leave space between the heading and the headline for the editor to write typesetting instructions.

Headline and body copy. Use a headline, with a three-line limit, to identify the story. Don't be concerned if the editor changes it. All body copy should be typed or computer-printed and double spaced. Answer the questions, *who*, *what*, *where*, *when*, *why*, and *how*, generally by the second paragraph, and complete necessary additional explanation by the end of the second page, if possible.

If a page is to be continued, place "more," centered at the bottom. At the top of the coninuation page, place key words of the headline on the left, followed by "(continued)," and place page number on the right. After the last line of the final page place "–END–," centered.

News release tips. You must overcome the editor's "So what?" or "Who cares?" reaction by immediately answering "What's the point of this release?" or identifying the readers who will be highly interested.

- Do not write, "My product is great." The release must read like news, not like an ad. And it must *be* news, not fluff.
- The release should contain absolutely accurate facts and should include opinions only of the persons quoted.
- If possible, find an independent endorser or distanced expert, such as a news broadcaster, disk jockey, editor, or customer you can quote to transmit the message.
- Use photos whenever they are available. Each photo should have a caption typed on a separate piece of paper and attached to the back of the photo with transparent tape, so that it can be read when looking at the photo. Include identifying data, in case the photo gets separated from the release.

NEWSLETTERS

Newsletters offer an excellent medium to provide additional exposure for messages you are communicating to other media. They should be perceived as goodwill or a public service. Unlike news releases, they let *you* control what is printed and when it is printed. They may be of any length and can be published on any schedule, but should be published regularly for effectiveness and credibility.

Your newsletter can be prepared in any style and composition, from photocopy to four-color composition. (Columns are easier to read than page-wide copy.) The local print shop can handle your copy. Or even better, do it in-house with desktop publishing software (see chapter 7).

SUMMARY

1. To make a sale, find out what your prospect wants or needs, package it so it fills a want or need, price it right, and get the prospect to inspect the package.
2. To beat the competition, you must make the customer perceive that your charter operation provides something special that no competitor offers. This something special is variously known as a "single most important tactic," a "unique selling proposition," or simply "a competitive advantage."
3. Operating without a database is like attempting to cross an ocean without charts.

4. AIDA (Attention, Interest, Desire, Action) will help create any ad.
5. The way to find out whether an advertising tool will work for your chartering business is to try it and measure the results.
6. A return-on-promotion formula provides a charter operator a single yardstick for measuring multiple advertising approaches.
7. Direct mail lets you measure results of every step of your promotion—your offer, its packaging, your mailing list, and the response rate.
8. Public relations gives a prospect the perception of legitimacy and credibility because it is not paid advertising.

CHAPTER 5

How to Write a Marketing Plan

Chapter 4 explained that when you use a marketing tool for advertising, you should measure the results in order to discover (1) which tools and which adaptations work best for *your* business, and (2) how to refine those that work so as to produce more sales per dollar spent. On a broader scope, a marketing plan serves the same purpose. You first formalize the plan logically in writing to ensure that you have not overlooked any factor affecting the marketing sequence. Then, as you go through actual marketing, you review the plan and measure it in terms of sales to see how well it is producing. At the end of a designated period (and sometimes sooner, in case of a sudden change), you modify it as necessary to improve it. Finally, your written plan becomes an educational document for managers and employees, to ensure that you are all steering the same course.

Because the marketing plan is used and revised so often, many businesses work with one or more copies separate from the business plan. However, the original is an integral chapter of the business plan.

The marketing plan may be prepared in any format that offers a logical conclusion to an evaluation of the factors affecting your marketing. The following format, which is used in this chapter, is a topical outline containing components adapted from Kotler.[1] It will be expanded, item by item, as the chapter progresses.

Executive Summary
Table of Contents
Opportunities and Threats
    Customers

Competitors
Market Share
Suppliers
Market Intermediaries
Publics
Demographic Factors
Economic Factors
Technological Factors
Political/Legal Factors
Social/Cultural Factors
Physical Factors

Company Strengths and Weaknesses

Marketing
Finance
Invention/Production
Organization

Issues Analysis

Objectives

Financial Objectives
Marketing Objectives

Possible Marketing Strategies

Target Market Determination
Positioning
Product Line
Pricing
Distribution Channels
Sales Force
Servicing
Timing
Advertising and Sales
Public Relations
Research and Development
Marketing Research

Action Programs

The Marketing Budget

Controls

As will be shown in the rest of this chapter, the outline is used to develop the following:

1. Opportunities and threats affecting my company.
2. Strengths and weaknesses the company can use to exploit the opportunities and minimize the threats.
3. Questions I must answer in order to exploit opportunities and minimize threats.
4. Measurable objectives that will answer those questions.
5. Marketing strategies that might accomplish those objectives.
6. What cost will be and what we should take in as profit.
7. How I can monitor the progress.

The executive summary is a brief overview of the plan. Your accountant or your lender will probably look here first. The table of contents is self explanatory. The following sections provide detailed information on the remaining items of the marketing plan.

OPPORTUNITIES AND THREATS

The subparagraphs in this section identify the major opportunities and threats that can affect the future of the business. Rank them in order, so that more attention will be paid to the earlier ones. Include suggestions for possible actions. Such actions will be analyzed later, along with company strengths and weaknesses, in the section on *issues analysis*.

Customers

Your customer profile will help your advertising reach prospects who are likely to behave just like your customers, right down to the point of buying a charter. Identify who your customers are, what they need and want, what their buying habits are, and the reason they buy from you. Clarify whether they are businesses, individuals, or agents. Describe whether they are local, regional, or international. Determine their age, sex, religion, marital status, family size, occupation, and income level.

Ascertain the size of the market in units or dollars, and add return customers. State whether the market is growing, steady, or decreasing. If it is growing, estimate the annual growth rate. Back up all statements in this section by describing the means you used to develop the information.

Competitors

Analyze each competitor's size, goals, market share, service or product quality, and marketing strategies. Outline your competitors' pricing, which ones are prosperous and why, which ones are barely getting by, which ones went out of business and why, and which ones have advantages that you don't. In your calculations, reserve a spot for indirect competition stemming from noncharter businesses that are competing with you for the customer's discretionary income.

Market Share

You can measure market share in four ways. Let's say you have a charter operation in the San Francisco Bay Area, and you consider the Bay Area to be your market. Your *overall market share* is your sales expressed as a percentage of state or national industry sales. *Served market share* is your sales expressed as a percentage of only the Bay Area market. *Market share relative to the top three competitors* (including you) is your sales as a percentage of the combined sales of the three largest competitors. *Market share relative to the leading competitor* is your sales as a percentage of the leading competitor's sales.

By inserting various figures into these formulas, you can see that four different levels of percentage emerge—and studying each might offer alternative strategies for increasing market share. In addition, comparing unit sales (numbers of charters or pieces of major merchandise) as well as dollar sales can provide yet another insight into how to expand market share.

Suppliers

Evaluate existing and potential suppliers, such as those that provide slips, moorings, lay-ups, and bareboat provisions. For your distributors, survey the percentage of sales via each channel of distribution, the motivation of dealers and distributors, and the possibility of adding, deleting, or modifying channels.

Market Intermediaries

Appraise the middlemen who aid you or could aid you in marketing. They include physical distribution firms, marketing service agencies, and financial intermediaries. Think about lenders, printers, candidates for cross-promotions (see chapter 4 on marketing tools), and other firms that can help you market.

Publics

Consider targeting public relations campaigns to groups with an actual or potential interest or impact upon the marketing sequence. Assess financial organizations, the media, government groups, activist groups, the general public, and specialized local groups that might aid or hinder your marketing.

Demographic Factors

Consider how your charter business could be affected by birth rates, population shifts, educational levels, ethnic mixes, and changes from mass markets to micromarkets.

Economic Factors

Anything that affects discretionary spending can have an impact upon the chartering industry. The devastating effect of the recession of the early 1980s on Gulf Coast marinas and the oil industry is an example. While cruising Louisiana waters in 1992, I was still finding unfinished marinas and abandoned sailboats. Besides the state of the economy, consider potential changes in incomes, savings rates, credit availability, and spending patterns.

Technological Factors

Decide how ongoing R&D (research and development), innovation, and potential technological breakthroughs will affect your chartering operation. Entrepreneurs who first exploited jet-powered water bikes had paid attention to this section of their marketing plans.

Political/Legal Factors

Evaluate current and pending legislation and regulations that can affect the business. If warranted, lay out options either to influence such activity or to avoid the results of it. As an example of how important this can be, during 1995 the Coast Guard proposed that each uninspected vessel carry a Category 1 (406 MHZ) Emergency Position–Indicating Radio Beacon. This would have cost charter operators using such vessels an estimated $1,350 to $1,500 per beacon. In response to lobbying by those affected, the Coast Guard withdrew the proposal.

Social/Cultural Factors

List core beliefs, secondary beliefs, changing cultural values, and subcultural values that can impact upon the business. A historical example of such a change is when the dive industry converted from its male-macho image to today's color-coordinated, socially interactive sport for divers of both sexes. Charter operators with marketing plans recognizing that men and women of all ages and various levels of physical ability wanted to dive—and could dive—moved their businesses into a new profit era.

Physical Factors

Consider the availability of needed raw materials and energy. Analyze pollution and environmental issues that might impinge upon the business. Analyze everything, from electricity brownouts during peak air-conditioning months to HAZMAT considerations (see chapter 3).

COMPANY STRENGTHS AND WEAKNESSES

As explained more fully in the chapter on marketing tools, your niche—the way you have positioned or differentiated the company—should offer a unique benefit that the customers need or want, but that no competitor can easily copy. Summarize it here.

Identify other strengths and weaknesses in marketing, finance, invention/production, and organization. The company's strengths should suggest possible strategies, while its weaknesses point to things to avoid or correct. These strengths and weaknesses will be analyzed along with opportunities and threats in the section on issues analysis.

Marketing

Insert a history of sales, prices, margins, and net profit for each major service and product. If you are computerized, preparing this will be a relatively simple spreadsheet exercise, which can be put in graph form for comparison of sales results.

Describe your marketing methods. If you are a mom-and-pop operation, you can simply summarize the marketing tools you are using (see chapter 4). However, if the company is large enough to have several departments, you should outline the way each department interplays in marketing.

For example, if a charter company has departments for advertising, brokerage, charter crews, and a sail school, each of these departments must be specifically addressed. Remember that one purpose of the marketing plan is to be sure that all hands are steering the same course.

Finance

Summarize the business's debt status, possibilities for future loans, and any other pertinent financial factors. This section might play a key part in the sections on issues analysis and financial objectives that follow.

Invention/Production

Review required items that your company can build, manufacture, repair, or otherwise create. Alternatively, determine the necessary creative functions for which it must seek outside vendors.

Organization

Assess organizational strengths and weaknesses in order to prepare for exploitation of the former and modification or acknowledgment of the latter in the section on issues analysis that follows.

ISSUES ANALYSIS

Use the findings from the opportunities-and-threats and strengths-and-weaknesses sections to define issues that will be resolved by the plan. In the sections that follow you will use these issues to develop objectives, marketing strategies, and action programs. Issues can be stated as questions, such as:

- Should the company expand its weekend charter business to weekdays?
- Should the company hire a second captain?

OBJECTIVES

This is the point in the plan where you convert the issues into measurable financial and marketing objectives. In order to be measurable, the objectives should be established for stated time periods.

Financial Objectives

Let's say that you have been managing to pay your sportfisherman's mortgage, maintenance, insurance, and dockage through weekend charters. You want to pay off the mortgage early and buy a second boat in order to retire from your landlubber job a few years down the road and be a full-time charterer. Your weekend charters are consistently sold out. However, your uncle, who taught you almost everything you know about fishing and boating, has agreed to skipper your boat on two weekdays for charter parties. Your marketing plan has shown that it would be unrealistic in your area to attract the same numbers of customers during the week as on weekends, but that there is a partial market to exploit. Here are examples of objectives that you might develop.

- Increase gross chartering income by 40 percent next year, and by an additional 10 percent during the following two years.

- Produce a cash flow of $XX,XXX next year, and $XX,XXX for each of the following two years.
- Produce net profits of $XX,XXX next year, and $XX,XXX for each of the following two years.

Marketing Objectives

Convert the financial objectives into marketing objectives, stated hierarchically, if possible. Lower-ranking objectives should be derived from higher-ranking objectives. Objectives should be obtainable but challenging. Here are examples from the scenario outlined above:

- For next year, sell XX weekday charters a month at promotional prices marked down 10 percent from standard weekend prices.
- For the following two years, sell XX plus XX weekday charters a month at promotional prices marked down 10 percent from standard weekend prices.
- Increase served market share of weekend sportfishing charters from 30 percent to 40 percent by selling Friday night fishing parties.

POSSIBLE MARKETING STRATEGIES

Review each tool that follows in order to determine a broad marketing strategy that will achieve the objectives. If revising the marketing plan, add new strategic efforts and retain ongoing ones to keep the plan complete.

Target Market Determination

You might be targeting your entire served market, or perhaps you are launching one or more separate campaigns aimed at portions of the market. Identify each market targeted.

In the example given, where the charter operator has decided to expand charters to a weekday market and to increase weekend sales by adding a Friday night fishing party at a party-boat price of $200, this section might be developed as follows:

> The weekday market comprises retired persons, younger persons who can afford to leave work during the week, and vacationers. Because the three groups have different wants and needs, advertising will be placed with media that have the best chance to reach all three groups and sales will be measured for each.

The market for Friday-night fishing party charters is parties (up to six) of people who do not own boats and who want to spend a Friday night out on the water with the boys. It is anticipated that such groups will be found in local companies such as (name companies you will target).

The market for Saturday and Sunday charters, which keeps the boat full on those days, will continue to be the served market.

Positioning

This section outlines positioning for either a special promotion or for the served market. For the example we are working on, the competitive situation might allow the charterer to position his boat as the *only* boat offering weekday charters, and the only boat available for thank-God-it's-Friday night fishing charters. The profitable positioning campaign for Saturdays and Sundays—"Return with fish to fry or your money back"—would continue.

Product Line

Answer key questions that a stranger might ask about your product or products. Explain why they are designed and packaged the way they are, and include proprietary rights information.

Pricing

You can establish pricing from an analysis of material costs, labor costs, operating expenses, planned profit, competitor prices, and your market share calculations. Initial cost figures must come from projections (also called pro forma statements), which are part of the financial plan (which becomes a separate chapter of the business plan). The projections will be replaced by costs from actual financial summaries (profit-and-loss statements) as they become available (see chapter 2). If you plan to offer credit card service, be sure to include its cost with your other costs.

Your accountant can use the financial data to help you set prices mathematically, but *you* must incorporate pricing into your plan as a marketing strategy. Are you selling quality charters with linen service, or cut-rate boat trips? Will you opt for everyday low prices, or do you want to keep a price cushion to allow for special discounts? Above all, what is your competition charging?

Distribution Channels

Explain how products and services will be made available to the customer. Will the customers come to the boat? Will you pick them up at a hotel? Will you sell catalog items from stock? Will you drop-ship?

Sales Force

Outline how the sales force will assist with each campaign. Account for employee time off, as well as for special holiday sales periods. Set time for employee training, if applicable.

Servicing

Explain how you will service the products you sell. For example, a dive operator might perform basic product servicing on the boat or in the shop and warranty servicing in the shop. A ship's store operator might have to determine how to handle returns for servicing.

Timing

State when you plan to enter the market or start the campaign and why that date is important. For example, you might introduce a new boat at the beginning of the season. Alternatively, you could put it into service in the middle of the season, *before* a competitor takes delivery on his or her new boat.

Advertising and Sales

This is the section where you match your positioning and target market with sales methods that will reach that market. You will be searching for good returns on promotion at costs that you judge will be within the budget resulting from this marketing plan. You should also plan for indirect (institutional) advertising that will pay off in the future. And don't forget less costly marketing tools, like bulletin boards and business cards (see chapter 4 for marketing tools and Appendix F for return on promotion and break-even analysis).

Obtain information from the media (including print shops that do direct-mail work) about the services and results they offer. From their rates, determine the amounts that charter operations similar to yours are spending on advertising. With this information analyzed, you can get a good handle on your competitors' advertising budget just by keeping track of their ads. Then make your own advertising decisions, being sure to attach a specific goal to each advertising activity. Record the results here, along with copies of rate sheets, promotional material, and schedules.

Public Relations

Make the opening of your business or the beginning of your campaign newsworthy (see chapter 4). Explain it in this section, and establish a news release plan. Include each newsworthy item, its date of release, and addresses of media.

Research and Development (R & D)

Indicate any research and development that is necessary for or would improve your marketing thrust. Include alternatives in case R & D goals do not materialize.

Marketing Research

For a small business operator, marketing research means more than spreadsheets, charts, and graphs prepared from thick reference documents. It means obtaining information from customers, prospects, prospects who did *not* buy, competitors, competitors' customers, and competitors' prospects who did not buy. It also means gathering data from associations and noncompeting businesses that interact with your customers and prospects. And it means finding out from your employees what your customers like and don't like about your charter service. The results of all of this, along with proposed further research projects, belong in this section.

ACTION PROGRAMS

Determine who will do what, when, and how much it will cost to accomplish each element of the marketing strategy. Remember that unless a program is listed here it probably will not be accomplished.

THE MARKETING BUDGET

Preparing a marketing budget from this *objectives and tasks* study is the most accurate of various methods available to establish a budget, and by this stage of marketing plan development it is relatively simple. The resulting document is essentially a cash-flow projection (see chapter 2). To prepare it, on the revenue side, list forecasted sales volume in charter numbers and product units and the anticipated average realized price. On the expense side, show cost of sales and the marketing costs. The difference is projected profit.

If the budget proves to be too high, cuts will have to be made by modifying either decisions made in the marketing plan sequence that led to the budgetary figures, or the methods outlined in the action programs, or both. In a mom-and-pop operation you probably will estimate and modify mostly as you work through the marketing plan. However, in a larger operation, you might complete the plan, send the budget (or entire document) to higher management for approval, and revise the marketing plan if the budget comes back with a markdown.

Once approved, the budget becomes the basis for implementing and monitoring the marketing plan.

CONTROLS

Use this section to specify control measures for monitoring the plan's progress. You will probably stipulate monthly or quarterly progress checks against the projection. You might also add contingency plans, outlining steps to take in response to specific adverse developments, such as hurricanes or typhoons, sinkings, or supplier nonperformance. And you certainly want to provide for testing the results, so that you can modify the plan at periodic intervals, or in case of contingencies.

SUMMARY

1. A marketing plan is like an advertisement, in that it can be created through logical reasoning, and its results can be measured.
2. A charter company can be either a ho-hum operation or it can fill a niche that draws customers who fit your customer profile.
3. Your niche is the way you have positioned or differentiated the company. Such positioning should offer a unique benefit that the customers need or want, but that no competitor can easily copy.
4. If your top two competitors have 20 percent of the market and you have 10 percent, your market share relative to them is 33.3 percent.
5. If your served market is five thousand charters per month and you are selling five hundred, your market share in unit sales is 10 percent.
6. When you have completed the action programs portion of the marketing plan, preparing the budget is simply a matter of making a cash-flow projection.

CHAPTER 6

How to Write a Business Plan

SCORE counselor Peter Olsen from St. Petersburg, Florida,[1] says, "Before you let your emotions crowd out reason, back off and start planning." He explains, "You've got to do a thorough business plan. Sleep on it for a little while, then review it, and do it again if necessary."

Let's expand Olsen's comment with advice from Mike McCrory, a dive-shop operator from Little Rock, Arkansas, in business since 1980:[2]

> Some people who like the sport of diving and think it's great fun decide to get into business. Then they change their minds, because they find that this is a full-time business, a retail business, very specialized, and highly competitive, a small niche. It is all based upon the customer's disposable income.

These quotes are reinforced by consistent statistics showing that more than 50 percent of all small businesses fail in the first year. Moreover, it generally takes five years before a charter operator can be sure of having a successful enterprise. The key to passing these one-year and five-year benchmarks is a business plan.

A business plan will do more than prevent you from failing. It is an inventory of all the trees that make up the forest, taken before the pressure of daily operations keeps you from seeing those trees. It will serve as an operational map and, as time goes on, as a historical aid, explaining how the business got where it is and where it is going. It is an excellent communications tool when you need to orient your employees and suppliers. It can be an important tool to help you convince the IRS you are indeed running a business. And it is an absolute necessity when you go for a loan.

Package the plan professionally, because it will be the best indicator to an outsider—be it lender or a possible new employee—of how to judge your potential for success. Keep it under forty pages. Include only the attachments that the specific reader needs to see, and keep the others with your personal copy. Have copies of the plan bound, or use a cover from the office supply store. Keep track of every copy, and if a loan is refused, retrieve that copy.

You can write your business plan by finding and recording the information needed to fill in the outline that follows.[3] Although the outline might appear intimidating at first, it meets the purpose of the plan, which is to present your concept in such precise detail that someone unfamiliar with boats and chartering could actually steal your ideas after reading it. Here is the outline:

- I. Cover Sheet
- II. Executive Summary
  - A. The Company
  - B. Objectives
  - C. Financing
- III. Table of Contents
- IV. The Industry
- V. The Company
  - A. Legal Structure
  - B. Your Business
  - C. Positioning
  - D. Location
  - E. Personnel
  - F. Record Keeping
- VI. The Insurance Plan
- VII. The Marketing Plan
- VIII. The Financial Plan
  - A. Summary of Financial Needs
  - B. Sources and Uses of Funds
  - C. Monthly Cash-Flow Statement (Cash Projection)
  - D. Three-Year Income Projection
  - E. Break-even Analysis
  - F. Profit-and-Loss Statement
  - G. Balance Sheet
  - H. Business Financial History
- IX. Attachments

The remainder of the chapter explains the topics listed in the outline.

COVER SHEET

The cover sheet serves as the title page. It should contain the name of the company; address; phone number; logo; names, titles, addresses, and phone numbers of owners; the date the plan was prepared; the name of the preparer, and the number of the copy.

EXECUTIVE SUMMARY

The Company

Summarize what the company is: its products and services, its positioning, and why it will be successful. Explain your chartering experience and, if you lack experience, how you plan to gain it. Attach a resume.

Objectives

List your goal or goals, such as:

- To achieve market share of XX percent of the estimated market of $XX in five years.
- To become the Bay Area's recognized experts in sportfishing by consistently enabling our clients to become tournament winners.
- To computerize all appropriate accounting, bookkeeping, and client database functions within two years.

Financing

If you need a loan, explain how much you need, why you need it, and how and when you plan to repay it. If you don't intend to take out a loan, explain why you made this decision.

THE INDUSTRY

Explain the overall industry as if you were writing to somebody who knows absolutely nothing about it. Describe whether it is young or mature, growing or declining. Discuss methods of pricing and discounting.

Summarize the scope and operations of the industry sector that affects your type of operation. For example, if you run a mom-and-pop charter, explain how such businesses operate. Or if you operate a dive boat, concentrate on the dive industry. Include current trends. Project how the industry may change, and what you plan to do about such change.

THE COMPANY

Legal Structure

Describe the legal structure you have chosen and why (see chapter 1). Attach copies of the partnership papers, corporate charter, or other documentation.

Your Business

Identify the business you are in. Describe whether your business is a charter company, a bareboat charterer, a brokerage firm, an agency, a resort, a dive shop, a fish camp, an excursion boat operation, a combination of several of these, or something else. Give the company's history, its present status, and its projected future. Outline the products and services the company offers, and those you plan to add in the future.

Positioning

Explain what makes the company different and gives it a competitive advantage. As discussed in chapter 4 on marketing tools, positioning springs from a single most important tactic or unique selling point. It provides something that the customer wants or needs and that the competition cannot easily copy. Captain Memo's Pirate Cruise, Inc., operating out of Clearwater Beach, Florida, is an example.[4] Here are summarized excerpts from the operators' full-color, slick, foldover flier:

> *The Vessel.* The *Pirate's Ransom* was custom designed and built for the owners in 1993. The 70′5″ vessel is certified by the Coast Guard to carry 125 passengers. It is powered by twin 671 Detroit Diesels of 235 horsepower each, with two Northern Lights 60-kilowatt generators.
>
> *The Crew.* The spirited pirates are individually selected by Captain Memo himself. They are chosen not only for their enthusiastic personalities and immeasurable politeness, but also for their knowledge of seamanship and expert capabilities. Panama Pam [author's note: Memo's wife], Typhoon Tom, Treacherous Trea, Limbo Larry, Cancun Charlie, and Jammin Joyce are anxious to meet you.

This scarlet and black three-master, equipped with a built-in professional sound system, replaced the charter operators' first pirate ship, which they once had lived aboard. It was a 30-foot sloop, painted black, with brown sails. Memo (formerly known as Bill Wozencraft) began his pirate career on that vessel when Pam made him some pantaloons, a bandanna, and a sash.

Location

Describe the location of your office and vessel and explain why you chose them.

Personnel

Prepare biographical sketches of the company's officers, with emphasis on their qualifications. Specify the duties of each and their benefits and other forms of compensation. Attach resumes.

Describe who the employees are, how they were selected, their responsibilities, and their wages.

List outside professional resources available (accountant, lawyer, insurance agent, lender), how they will be used, and the recompense.

Describe any gaps in officer or employee skill requirements and how you will fill them.

Record Keeping

Describe the accounting system you will use or are using, and the person or firm that will do the record keeping. List the location and types of business bank accounts (see chapters 1 and 2).

THE INSURANCE PLAN

Insert the insurance plan developed from chapter 3.

THE MARKETING PLAN

Insert the marketing plan developed from chapter 5.

THE FINANCIAL PLAN

Among the documents discussed below, the cash-flow statement (budget), three-year income projection, and break-even analysis are pro forma projections. If your business is new, completion of them will conclude the financial plan. If the business is established, add the remaining performance statements listed: balance sheet, income (profit-and-loss) statement, and business financial history.

- *Summary of Financial Needs.* Indicate why you are applying for a loan and how much you need.

- *Sources and Uses of Funds.* List fixed assets and working capital requirements and their sources. Sources might be personal savings, from profits (accounts receivable), vendor credit, currently owned (such as truck or boat), installment purchase, personal cash, existing loan, needed loan, or others.
- *Monthly Cash-Flow Statement (Cash Projection).* This is a one-year, pro forma projection (see chapter 2).
- *Three-Year Income Projection.* This is a pro forma statement showing your projections for three years beyond the budget year (see chapter 2).
- *Break-even Analysis.* Examples of preparing this pro forma statement are shown in chapter 2 and in appendix F on return on promotion and break-even analysis.
- *Profit-and-Loss Statement.* See chapter 2 on accounting and budgeting.
- *Balance Sheet (Net Worth Statement).* See chapter 2 on accounting and budgeting.
- *Business Financial History.* If you are applying for a loan, attach the application and reference it here. Otherwise, summarize financial information about the company from its start to the present.

ATTACHMENTS

Attach the supporting documents for the three main parts of the business plan: the company, the marketing plan, and the financial data. Examples are:

- Short personal resumes
- Personal financial statement of owner. (If you are a new business owner, this will be part of your financial section.)
- Credit reports
- Copies of leases
- Letters of reference (business and personal)
- Contracts
- Other legal documents
- Other documents referred to in the plan

CHAPTER 7

Computer Assistance

Aboard a boat you might use a block, a winch, a capstan, a come-along, or any other leveraging device that will produce the mechanical advantage you need for a particular job. In the office you can use another leveraging device the size of a bread box, so technologically advanced that its predecessor once filled an entire building.

This electronic marvel can produce business plans, customer databases, desktop-published advertisements, and bookkeeping and accounting spreadsheets. Your computer can almost instantly recall the birth date, children's names, or other personal data that will please a customer who calls. Your computer can keep your to-do file and handle your appointment calendar. It can record and sort your Global Positioning System (GPS) or Loran waypoints for fishing holes, dive sites, sea buoys, and anchorages. It can even bring in weather synopses.

When running a charter business, you should ask constantly, "Can I do this function quicker, more accurately, or less expensively by computer?" And if the answer is yes, you should go through the steps outlined in this chapter to decide whether to computerize that part of the business. If you don't do so, you can bet your bimini that your competition will.

If you aren't using computer assistance, read this chapter carefully. If you are, skim over it for new ideas. It covers everything just mentioned and more.

LEARNING ABOUT COMPUTERS

I bought my first computer ten years ago with income from a stormy transatlantic delivery. After completing the crossing in better condition than the 46-foot ketch, I decided that anybody who could sail across an ocean ought to be able to tackle a computer. So I splurged on a little gray electronic box with monitor.

Five computers later, I can attest that, slowly but surely, I learned to use every business application that was bundled with that first computer—word processing, spreadsheet, database, and more. In doing so, I also learned the following undeniable, absolute truths:

- A computer will never blow you to smithereens if you punch the wrong button. But it will lose data if you don't back up your files once in a while. Everybody I know who has lost files due to a computer crash neglected to copy them for days, weeks—even months.
- Don't expect to learn as much about a computer in an hour as you have learned about boats over years and years. But you can start the way you did with boats: You can learn how to turn on the machine, set a simple course, check some instruments while under way, and return. Once you can do that, you can build on this knowledge by adding courses, one at a time.
- Don't waste time fighting the language. If the documentation says "Press the carriage return key" and the key on your keyboard reads, "Enter," press Enter.
- Before deciding you can afford to spend the rest of your life as a computer-*illiterate* charter operator, read a book or two or attend a weekend seminar—and don't worry about the parts you don't understand. Your knowledge will grow. A humorous, easy-to-read book that can get you started and keep you going is the latest edition of *The Secret Guide to Computers*, by Russ Walter.[1] Walter also offers weekend "blitz" courses and even invites phone calls and visits.
- You can almost always accomplish a task on a computer several different ways, but you don't have to learn every one of them.
- As a corollary to the above, computers and software can do more than you will ever want them to do. As a charter operator, you need an overview of what they *can* do, but only have time to learn what *you want* them to do for your business.

To assist with the last undeniable, absolute truth, the remainder of the chapter follows a logical overview of (1) software applications and operating systems, and (2) preparing your shopping list.[2]

SOFTWARE APPLICATIONS AND OPERATING SYSTEMS

The most common applications are programs for word processing, databases, spreadsheets, accounting, graphics, desktop publishing, and communications by telephone (via a modem or fax modem). Integrated programs contain several of these applications in a single package, generally at a lower price than if the applications were bought separately.

Word Processing

Word processors create and store written data in the form of electronic documents, allowing users to insert and delete words, sentences, and paragraphs at will. They might include spell checkers, thesauruses, and grammar checkers. If you use a word processor, never again will you or your secretary need to retype an entire letter or form to make a small correction. Just make the correction on the computer, and push a key to reprint the document.

Databases

Anything you can file on a three-by-five card (or five-by-seven or just about any other size) can become a record in a database. Fields in the records can be sorted, selected, counted, retrieved, and even used with a word processor's form letter for direct-mail addressing.

You can use the information in a database for personalized marketing as well as for developing a customer profile (see chapters 1, 5, and 6). You can quickly identify birth dates, personal preferences, chartering history, and the other variables you want in your customer profile. You can target those variables in voluminous direct-marketing mailouts or even simple handwritten letters.

You might keep a database called up as a handy Rolodex file for phone numbers and fax numbers. In many databases, a click or a keystroke on a number automatically dials the number, saving time and eliminating the chance for error when manually dialing.

As mentioned earlier, a database of GPS or Loran waypoints also might save time and provide accuracy. I've used mine to print out waypoints when making deliveries through areas away from my home cruising grounds. I just have the computer select the latitudes and longitudes where I'm cruising and command the computer to print the results. Conversely, this method keeps the GPS printout for my local operating area small, handy, and legible.

Of course, many charter operators won't need GPS databases. As with all applications, use only what will increase *your* productivity or reduce *your* overhead, and never launch a program just because it's there.

Spreadsheets

Spreadsheets organize financial information, inventory, and other quantifiable information, so that it can be analyzed, altered for "what if" purposes, and put in graph form for easy visual comparisons. Spreadsheets and accounting programs (described below), can eliminate the need for manual adding, subtracting, multiplying, dividing, or advanced calculating.

Some charter operators find that a full-blown accounting program is a case of the tail wagging the dog; they just don't need that much of a system. So, depending upon the size and type of your chartering operation, you might decide to create an accounting and bookkeeping system with your spreadsheet program.

The financial statements discussed in chapter 2, i.e., profit-and-loss statement, expenses as percentages of sales, break-even analysis, balance sheet, monthly cash projection, and income projection, will adapt easily to a spreadsheet application, and most spreadsheet applications allow for linking spreadsheets. For example, a change in an inventory spreadsheet can automatically change the inventory values on the balance sheet.

Spreadsheets also take the drudgery out of measuring the results of direct-mail marketing (see section on return on promotion in chapter 4 and see appendix F).

Accounting

If you are more comfortable with an application that leads you step by step and automatically links reports and spreadsheets, you might opt for an off-the-shelf accounting program.

Accounting programs can monitor the records and budgeting procedures outlined in the chapter on accounting and budgeting. They can also manipulate your inputs so that the resulting reports are ready at the stroke of a key. How could any business operator ever have afforded the labor costs to manually enter and cross-reference those ancient green forms that have been replaced by automatic calculations and automatic printouts?

Graphics

Graphics programs allow you to create and manipulate graphs and drawings for newsletters, posters, advertisements, and similar documents. Some provide for importing photographs or create animated pictures for multimedia presentations.

Desktop Publishing

These programs combine word processing with graphics programs to create newsletters, manuals, fliers, advertisements, magazines, and newspapers. Desktop publishing lets you avoid costs for layout and pasteup. If you buy an ink jet or bubble jet printer (for well under five hundred dollars), you can prepare camera-ready masters and have those masters copied at a nearby discount small-business supply center for prices unheard of until just this decade.

Communications

Communications software uses your computer's modem (or fax modem) to reach other computers similarly equipped. Once connected, you can "talk" via keyboard and can upload and download files. You can communicate by direct telephone call or connect to bulletin board systems (BBSs) and commercial on-line services. Most BBSs and on-line services offer file uploads and downloads, as well as forums, where people with similar interests can communicate, and terminals for electronic mail (e-mail).

Of special importance to charter operators is the Small Business Administration's *SBA Online*. This BBS provides a gateway to other federal systems and to the Internet (more later). In addition to other services, SBA Online offers three levels of access for file uploads and downloads. A toll-free number connection lists nineteen downloadable file categories. A 900-number connection and a 202-number connection list ten more categories. You can also connect with SBA Online via your own Internet access at sbaonline.sba.gov. See appendix G, SBA Online, for more information.

Nobody knows how many millions of people and thousands of terminals use the Internet. This national and international net can provide e-mail service to anybody who has access to the Internet or the major commercial on-line services. You can use the Internet if you are connected with universities, government agencies, or businesses that have access. You also can use it for a fee through on-line services. Some of the commercial on-line services are America Online, CompuServe, Delphi, GEnie, and Prodigy.

PREPARING YOUR SHOPPING LIST

In Office Depot's *How to Computerize Your Small Business*,[3] Bryan Pfafenberger provides some of *his* undeniable, absolute truths. Here is an adaptation:

- Buying a computer without knowing what you are going to do with it makes as much sense as hiring a captain without knowing what you want a captain to do.
- Placing a computer on your desk and continuing to operate BC (before computers) will never, ever, improve your productivity.
- Trying to computerize your business all at once is like trying to correct an engine failure without isolating the problem.

Putting these truths together, here is a minimal-cost, no-upheaval method of using computer assistance:

1. Identify one problem with the operation of your charter business that might be alleviated by computer.
2. Once you have identified the problem, find the right software to correct the problem.
3. Select an operating system, computer, and other hardware that the software can use. If you have found software for more than one set of hardware, select the hardware that will give you the most flexibility for future expansion.
4. When you have mastered the software and solved the problem, build your expertise by tackling another problem. An example follows.

Identify a Problem

Let's say that when Captain Charterhouse was planning the start of his business, he identified the old typewriter in his closet as a potential problem. Deciding to forego manual typing, he selected a word processing application and a PC operated by a DOS operating system. He eschewed Windows because at that time it was not bundled, and would have been an additional expense. A 16-pin dot matrix printer completed his hardware inventory, enabling him to handle correspondence, basic advertising copy, and rudimentary direct-mail marketing.

At the outset, his partner did the bookkeeping manually and provided numbers to their accountant once a quarter. However, as the business grew, his partner had to work more and more on the boat. Consequently, Captain Charterhouse hired a neighbor to do the bookkeeping.

During a semiannual review of the business plan, Captain Charterhouse noted that a spreadsheet program would cut bookkeeping costs considerably. Moreover, the time involved to operate a spreadsheet application would be insignificant compared to the original manual system.

Although it would cost more than a shareware program that was his alternative choice, Captain Charterhouse chose to buy one of the better-known spreadsheet programs because it provided more flexibility for additional use later.

The Captain selected the Windows version of the spreadsheet program because the vendor offered the program bundled with Windows. He believes that Windows will soon make DOS programs obsolete, so he considers this an ideal opportunity to move into the Windows environment.

His computer needs no upgrading to operate with Windows, because he purchased enough RAM to handle Windows when he bought the computer, and he already has an installed mouse. His printer will reproduce the spreadsheets and associated graphics satisfactorily for the time being, although he expects to upgrade to an ink jet printer when he starts producing fliers. For the present, however, he needs no additional hardware.

SUMMARY

1. A charter operator who refuses to use some form of computer assistance is like a skipper who refuses to use Loran or GPS. The job gets done, but the competition will be doing it quicker and more accurately.
2. Learning to use computers is like learning to use boats. Do it one step at a time.
3. To develop a shopping list, identify a problem, find the right software, and select hardware to run the software.
4. Like buying a boat, when buying a computer, buy enough power to allow for flexibility and expansion, but don't overdo it.

be issued with a *limited coastwise* endorsement for use in connection with oil-spill prevention and recovery. All six endorsements are explained below.

1. A *registry* endorsement authorizes foreign trade, including trade with Guam, American Samoa, Wake, Midway, and Kingman Reef. Registry does not allow the vessel to fish commercially in the navigable waters of the United States or in the Exclusive Economic Zone (EEZ—the zone of exclusive American fishing rights, up to 200 miles offshore), to trade in the Great Lakes, or to engage in coastwise trade.[3] (However, see section on "cruises-to-nowhere" later in the chapter.) Documentation for registry is available to both American-built *and* foreign-built vessels.
2. A *coastwise* endorsement entitles the vessel to employment in unrestricted coastwise trade, dredging, and towing. "Coastwise trade" is the transportation of passengers and merchandise between U.S. ports, including Puerto Rico and the U.S. Virgin Islands, on routes which are not more than 20 nautical miles offshore. The endorsement does not permit the vessel to conduct foreign trade, Great Lakes coastwise trade, or commercial fishing in the navigable waters of the United States or in the EEZ. A coastwise endorsement normally is authorized only for American-built vessels. In addition, a coastwise endorsement is *not* normally available to any vessel that has ever been foreign owned.
3. A *Great Lakes* endorsement entitles the vessel to engage in coastwise trade (carrying of passengers and merchandise in and out of Great Lakes ports) and towing on the Great Lakes. It does not allow the vessel to conduct foreign trade, coastwise trade other than on the Great Lakes, or fishing in the navigable waters of the United States, the EEZ, or the Great Lakes. A Great Lakes endorsement normally is available only for American-built vessels. In addition, Great Lakes documentation is *not* normally available to any vessel that has ever been foreign owned.
4. A *fishery* endorsement entitles the vessel to conduct commercial fishing in the navigable waters of the United States and in the EEZ, subject to federal and state laws regulating the fisheries. A fishery endorsement normally is available only to boats made in the United States and, with certain exceptions, boats which are American owned.[4]
5. A *recreational* endorsement entitles a vessel to pleasure use only. An uninspected vessel with this endorsement may be bareboat chartered for recreational use by charter parties of not more than twelve passengers.[5] The boat may be either American or foreign built.

6. A *limited coastwise* endorsement entitles a vessel to train for, implement, or support oil-spill cleanup operations on the navigable waters of the United States and in the EEZ. The endorsement, on a certificate of documentation form CG-1270, allows for a special citizenship status, referred to as an 883-1 citizen or 883-1 corporation, for owners of such vessels.[6]

All six types of endorsements require that the vessel measure at least 5 net tons, that the owner be a U.S. citizen, and that with certain exceptions for bareboat charters, the vessel be commanded by a U.S. citizen. However, see a later section in this chapter concerning the word *command*. (Also see an explanation of net tonnage later in the chapter.)

The term *owner* includes an individual, a partnership, an association, a joint venture, a trust, a corporation, or a governmental entity. In multiple ownerships, all principals must be U.S. citizens. In a corporation, this means the chief executive officer, chairman of the board, and a majority of the number of directors necessary to constitute a quorum.

Exceptions to the American-built and American-flagged requirements described above are possible for vessels that the courts adjudge to fit provisions of the law covering wrecked, forfeited, or captured vessels. Another possible exception is for vessels granted coastwise trading privileges by special congressional legislation.

The wrecked/forfeited/captured exceptions stem from the following rationale: (1) the early Congress felt that if an American captain should capture a European-built or foreign-owned privateer, the vessel should be exempted; (2) the lawmakers deemed the same in the case of foreign-built ships that might go aground on our shores and be recovered by Americans; and (3) they included in their exceptions foreign-built vessels that our courts might declare forfeited.

Don't overlook the provision for exception by special legislation. A reader told me that he had bought a boat that he was preparing to put into charter and then had bought a copy of *Charter Your Boat for Profit*. He learned from the book that his vessel would require documentation, but that it didn't fit the "all-American" rule for documentation. Catch-22? No. He told me that he had contacted his congressman, who had carried through the special legislation required for an exception. He added that he was calling to thank me for the information in the book.

A key exception to the all-American rule for coastwise trade concerns charter operators in the U.S. Virgin Islands. Commercial boats operating within the U.S. Virgins *do not* have to be American built, American owned, or American flagged. Hence, an owner of any mechanically propelled vessel operating in the Virgins has all three options for flagging: number it with the state (Virgin Islands), obtain documentation for registry from the Coast Guard, or obtain a foreign registry.

Now for the business of "command." Subpart L of Part 67 of the Code of Federal Regulations (CFR) 46, which establishes regulations for documentation, states that a certificate of documentation becomes invalid immediately when "The vessel is placed under the command of a person who is not a citizen of the United States."[7] Unfortunately, the CFR doesn't explain what "command" means. The courts have upheld cases wherein the owner (licensed or unlicensed) could hire a licensed non-American captain, as long as the owner remained on board—and in command. The crux of each of these cases seems to depend upon whether the owner could prove to the court that he or she was competent to handle the boat. This would imply that an owner who was competent enough to overrule the captain was, in fact, in command.

Net tonnage refers to the enclosed cubic feet of airspace available for cargo and passengers after all other space needed to operate the boat has been subtracted. One net ton is considered to be 100 cubic feet. Net tonnage is calculated by a complex measuring system called *admeasurement*, which traditionally had to be done by an official measurer. However, under CFR 46, Part 67 (1993), if your boat is 79 feet or shorter, Coast Guard reviewing personnel may calculate net tonnage for you.

In addition, you may estimate your net tonnage by using relatively simple formulas.[8]

When Does a Charter Operator Have a Choice in Documenting?

If your boat measures at least 5 net tons, does not have to be inspected, and you plan to carry on foreign trade, you have the option of either documenting for registry or flagging foreign. If she is at least 5 net tons and you plan to do only bareboat chartering for recreation, you may either document for recreation or obtain a state number.

Power vessels (monohull): $\frac{\text{length} \times \text{breadth} \times \text{depth} \times \ 67}{100}$

Sail vessels (monohull): $\frac{\text{length} \times \text{breadth} \times \text{depth} \times .50}{100}$

As a guide, a 26-foot monohull boat is often used as an example of 5-net tons.

Fig. 8-1. Estimating net tonnage

Cruises-to-Nowhere

The Bureau of Customs has determined that a vessel that goes beyond 3 miles, stops at no ports, does no fishing, and returns to its original berth is not engaging in coastwise trade. This allows a vessel over 5 net tons that carries and returns passengers to be either documented for registry or foreign-flagged. Remember that a vessel that is documented for registry does *not* have to be American built, and that a foreign-flagged vessel can be foreign-owned and foreign-built and can be commanded by a foreign citizen.

These "cruises-to-nowhere" have been used to ferry passengers out to gamble, watch whales, and observe missile launchings. You might find an adaptation of this exception that will fit your charter operation planning. However, check with the nearest Coast Guard marine safety office for the latest rulings. And if there is any doubt, be sure to get something in writing from the Coast Guard.

Advantages and Disadvantages of Documentation

If you have a choice as to whether to number or document, your selection of one over the other will depend upon how it affects the ease and cost of doing business. The comments that follow can help you decide.

Prior to 1963, there were no state titling laws, so documentation was the only practical way to get a loan to purchase a large boat. Documentation made the vessel the subject of a preferred ship's mortgage under the Ship Mortgage Act of 1920.

Today, thirty states have turned to boat titling laws that include reciprocity. The federal Vessel Identification System (VIS) (scheduled to commence April 1996), which includes guidelines for State Vessel Titling Systems (SVTS), adds strength to state titling by conferring preferred ship's mortgage status on vessels that meet the requirements of VIS and SVTS.[9] Therefore, more and more charter operators are simply buying and financing their boats just like they buy and finance automobiles—through their state systems. If you will be doing business in a title state, documentation may offer no advantage when applying for a loan. However, check with your lender before deciding between documentation and state numbering.

Watch out for the unexpected. American Airlines captain J. W. ("Bill") Kingsley bought a state-numbered Ericson 35 on Lake Texoma, on the Texas-Oklahoma border, and had no problem with a loan. A year later, he notified the bank that he was thinking of removing the boat from the lake, only to be told, "Not unless you document it." The loan officer didn't want the boat to leave the lake and sail the seven seas without a certificate of documentation showing the bank as lien holder.

Another factor that can pop up like a drifting buoy is that a documented vessel generally must be under command of an American citizen. Also, think ahead to the day you will want to sell. Will the prospective buyer, *and lender*, want the boat to be documented? Conversely, does your sales market include a high percentage of foreigners, who cannot own a documented vessel?

Now for two tales that hang around like a welcoming committee on the docks: First, it has been said that a certificate of documentation may simplify customs and immigration formalities in foreign ports. However, none of the charter operators queried for this book provided an example to support this.

Second, it has been said that a certificate of documentation makes a boat an extension of the U.S. government and that, should the boat be confiscated by a foreign power, the might of the U.S. government will come to the rescue. Well, if the government should contemplate sending a carrier battle group to rescue an American charter boat today, the ultimate decision would probably have little to do with whether the boat was documented or state-numbered.

When *Must* a Charter Operator Document?

You will need documentation if your boat measures 5 net tons or more and you intend to do any operations other than bareboating for recreation. Here is why:

> Any vessel of at least 5 net tons which engages in the fisheries on the navigable waters of the United States or in the Exclusive Economic Zone, Great Lakes trade, or coastwise trade, unless exempt under 67.9(c), must have a Certificate of Documentation bearing a valid endorsement appropriate for the activity in which engaged.[10]

Exempted by 67.9(c) are non-self-propelled vessels legally carrying on coastwise trade within a harbor, on U.S. rivers or inland lakes, or on the internal waters or canals of any state.

The term, *navigable waters of the United States*[11] means:

- The territorial seas
- All internal waters subject to tidal influence
- Other internal waters that have ever been used or *might* be used for navigation, regardless of man-made obstructions, such as bridges or dams
- Waters that a qualified body (governmental or otherwise) determines suitable for conversion to navigation

Each Coast Guard district keeps a list and charts depicting navigable waters. Contact the office of the district commander to arrange to see a copy, or send the geographic coordinates of the body of water that concerns your operation. Although the waters listed above might appear to include every last puddle in the country, the Coast Guard can rule (and Congress can declare) a body of water either navigable or nonnavigable.

Penalties

What happens if you don't document when you should? Title 46 U.S. Code, Section 12110(c), essentially says that if you are carrying passengers or cargo in a vessel that is supposed to be documented for that purpose, and it isn't, the U.S. government can seize it and require forfeiture of the vessel and its equipment. Unless you are found innocent in court, the only way you could get your boat back would be to buy it—as the highest bidder at auction. The section also authorizes civil penalties. Vessels involved in any other illegal activities, such as transporting drugs, are also subject to seizure and forfeiture.

How to Document

In 1994 the Coast Guard took steps to simplify bureaucratic red tape in the documentation process. The new system generally requires only two Coast Guard forms. Moreover, unlike in the past, inadvertent omissions do not necessarily automatically void an application.

In 1995, in order to further streamline the maintenance of a database of over two hundred thousand commercial and recreational vessels involving two hundred and forty thousand transactions annually, the Coast Guard centralized documentation operations. The new office handles documentation previously handled by fourteen separate ports of documentation. The telephone number is 1-800-799-8362. The address is:

U.S. Coast Guard
National Vessel Documentation Center
2039 Stonewall Jackson Drive
Falling Waters, WV 25419-4502

To document your boat, you may hire an agent or you may do it yourself. You will need to submit two copies of:

1. Application for Initial Issue of Documentation, Exchange or Replacement of Certificate of Documentation, or Redocumentation (CG-1258, revised 9-92 or later).
2. Evidence of Title, Bill of Sale (CG-1340, revised 9-92 or later), or a Builder's Certificate or equivalent records in the chain of title.

The first form (CG-1258) has a multiple title, because it also can be used to change existing documentation and even to *undocument* your boat. Just call or write the National Vessel Documentation Command for copies of each.

Here are some points to keep in mind when documenting:

- The Coast Guard uses its own bill-of-sale form (CG-340) merely as proof of ownership. It doesn't care what was paid for the boat. Although it will accept a phrase such as "ten dollars and other considerations" as the purchase price, this does not relieve the buyer of paying a state tax. Owners of documented vessels have found out the hard way that the states will collect tax money by obtaining Coast Guard records of documentation under the Freedom of Information Act and tracing the owners for delinquent taxes.
- It doesn't matter to the Coast Guard whether other boat names are similar or identical to yours. However, a boat name may not be spelled like or be phonetically like any word used to solicit assistance at sea. Neither may it be a word that is obscene, indecent, profane, or a word that might suggest a racial or ethnic slur.
- If you want to list a mailing address using a post office box, the box number and a street address must be listed on the application form.
- The hailing port you select must be in the United States and must, in general, be recognized by the U.S. Postal Service as a mailing address.
- A documented vessel must be marked on the stern with its name and hailing port in the Latin alphabet and/or arabic or roman numerals. If the boat is documented commercially, the name must also be on both bows. All markings must be at least 4 inches high.
- When you get your documentation certificate, you will receive an *official number*. A copy of this number, preceded by the abbreviation "NO.," must be placed inside the hull on some clearly visible structural part. It must be displayed in block-type arabic numerals not less than 3 inches in height. It must be permanently affixed so that it will be obvious if any alteration, removal, or replacement has taken place.
- Renewal must be done annually, normally by signing and returning the form that the Coast Guard sends to your mailing address.
- The fee for initial documentation with a registry endorsement is currently $133, a coastwise endorsement is $162, and a recreational endorsement is $133.
- If you use an agent, current fees run from $150 to $400.

Hints for Buying and Selling

In order to verify the status of the vessel's title, a copy of the Abstract of Title (CG-1332), as well as a Certificate of Ownership (CG-1330) setting forth ownership and encumbrances, can be obtained directly from the documentation center. The fee for the former is $25 and for the latter is $125.

FOREIGN REGISTRY

Depending upon where you will operate your charter business, the origins of your boat, and other variables discussed in this chapter, you might opt for foreign registry. If you are considering foreign registry, you should consult the appropriate country's regulations or hire an agent.

SUMMARY

1. Boat licensing must be either by state numbering, U.S. documentation, or foreign registry. You may have a choice, but if the boat you put into charter service measures over 5 net tons and will be used commercially on navigable U.S. waters, expect to document.
2. For general documentation requirements, see figure 8-2.
3. Some exceptions to general documentation requirements: bareboat charters for recreation, cruises-to-nowhere, operating in the U.S. Virgin Islands.
4. Navigable U.S. waters: most waters are navigable. Coast Guard district offices have lists and charts. Determinations of navigability can change.

	American built?	Owner American?	Commanded by American?	Mandatory if 5 NT
Registry	No	Yes	Yes	No
Coastwise (a)	Yes	Yes	Yes	Yes
Great Lakes (a)	Yes	Yes	Yes	Yes
Fishery	Yes	Yes	Yes	Yes
Pleasure	No	Yes	Yes	No

Note a. Coastwise and Great Lakes documentation not available if your vessel *ever* owned by a non-U.S. citizen or *ever* foreign-flagged.

Fig.. 8-2. General documentation requirements

- Whether you will charter the vessel with crew, will charter it without crew, or will not charter it (sell head spaces or tickets)

In order to carry out some of these operations, the vessel will have to be spected. This leads to the three types of vessels that the PVSA defines: *ssenger vessels*, *small passenger vessels*, and *uninspected passenger vessels*. oats defined as "passenger vessels" and "small passenger vessels" must be nspected. Obviously, an uninspected passenger vessel does not.

A practical understanding of these terms will provide guidelines for contracting bareboat and crewed charters, as well as for selling spaces for head boats, party boats, excursion boats, or any other kind of money-making boats (see also "Passenger Capacities for Inspected Vessels" in chapter 10).

What Is a Passenger?

A passenger is any person carried on the vessel except the owner or the owner's representative, the master, a paid crew member, or other persons employed or engaged in any capacity on board the vessel in the business of that vessel. In the case of a vessel under charter, an individual charterer (person contracting and/or receiving the money) or individual representative of the charterer is not a passenger.[2]

On a sailing-school vessel, also excluded from the definition of a passenger are:

- An employee of the owner of the vessel engaged in the business of the owner, except when the vessel is operating under a demise charter (see pages 123–24);
- An employee of the demise charterer of the vessel engaged in the business of the demise charterer;
- A sailing-school instructor or sailing-school student.

What Is a Passenger for Hire?

A passenger for hire is "a passenger for whom consideration is contributed as a condition of carriage on the vessel, whether directly or indirectly flowing to the owner, charterer, operator, agent, or any other person having an interest in the vessel."[3]

What Is Consideration?

Consideration is "an economic benefit, inducement, right or profit including pecuniary payment accruing to an individual, person, or entity, but not including a voluntary sharing of the actual expenses of the voyage, by monetary contribution or donation of fuel, food, beverage, or other supplies."[4]

CHAPTER 9

Bareboat or Crewed?
The Passenger Vessel Safety Act

OVERVIEW

The Passenger Vessel Safety Act of 1993 (PVSA)[1] established new standa of controlling bareboat and crewed charters. In doing this, it revised th definitions of passengers, passengers for hire, bareboat charters, crewed charters, and types of vessels. The result is a list of charter operations that each type of vessel may undertake.

Before the PVSA took effect, more than five hundred uninspected vessels were being used for bareboat chartering with relatively large numbers of customers aboard. Their status under the PVSA is discussed near the end of this chapter, in order to assist charter operators who might consider buying one of these vessels. In order to simplify the PVSA, this chapter outlines the definitions, summarizes the impact, and lists general examples. As part of the summary, the chapter provides a checklist in the form of figures 9-1 and 9-2, which were extracted from Navigation and Vessel Inspection Circular (NVIC) No. 7-94, "Guidance on the Passenger Vessel Safety Act of 1993." Use figure 9-1 if the boat is under 100 gross tons, and figure 9-2 if it is 100 gross tons or more.

This chapter can be an invaluable aid in decision making, but readers should query a Coast Guard marine safety office before making any operational decision affected by the PVSA about which they are not absolutely certain.

Under the PVSA, the charter operations you can undertake with your boat depend upon:

- Your vessel's gross tonnage
- The number of passengers your vessel will be carrying
- Whether the vessel will be used to carry passengers for hire

What Is a Passenger Vessel?

A passenger vessel is a vessel of at least 100 gross tons that is:

- Carrying more than twelve passengers, including at least one passenger for hire; or
- Chartered and carrying more than twelve passengers; or
- A submersible vessel carrying at least one passenger for hire.

What Is a Small Passenger Vessel?

A small passenger vessel is a vessel of less than 100 gross tons that is:

- Carrying more than six passengers, including at least one passenger for hire; or
- Chartered with the crew provided or specified by the owner or the owner's representative and carrying more than six passengers; or
- Chartered with no crew provided or specified by the owner or the owner's representative and carrying more than twelve passengers; or
- A submersible vessel carrying at least one passenger for hire.

What Is an Uninspected Passenger Vessel?

An uninspected passenger vessel is described as follows:
If it is at least 100 gross tons, it is a vessel that is:

- Carrying not more than twelve passengers, including at least one passenger for hire; or
- Chartered with the crew provided or specified by the owner or the owner's representative and carrying not more than twelve passengers.

If it is less than 100 gross tons, it is a vessel that is:

- Carrying not more than six passengers, including at least one passenger for hire; or
- Chartered with the crew provided or specified by the owner or the owner's representative and carrying not more than six passengers.

THE IMPACT OF THE REGULATIONS

An uninspected passenger vessel of less than 100 gross tons must be commanded by either a Coast Guard–licensed master or an operator of uninspected vessels. If it is chartered as a bareboat (no crew provided or specified by the owner or the owner's representative), the charter party may provide its own captain, either licensed or unlicensed. If it is a bareboat charter, the size of the charter party is limited to twelve.

An uninspected passenger vessel of 100 gross tons or more must be commanded by a Coast Guard–licensed master. If it is chartered as a bareboat (no crew provided or specified by the owner or the owner's representative), the charter party may provide its own captain, either licensed or unlicensed. If it is a bareboat charter, the size of the charter party is limited to twelve.

As mentioned earlier, the terms *passenger vessel* and *small passenger vessel* mean that such vessels must be inspected, with a current certificate of inspection. The certificate of inspection states the total number of persons that may be carried and describes the vessel, the route the vessel may travel, the minimum manning requirements, the safety equipment and appliances required to be on board, and the names of the owners and operators. All inspected vessels, whether or not under charter, must be commanded by a Coast Guard-licensed master (see chapter 10 for more information about passenger capacities for inspected vessels).

If a passenger vessel or a small passenger vessel is not inspected, with a current certificate of inspection, it may be seized and held for being used illegally. Furthermore, if any vessel is operated in variance with the definition, e.g., an uninspected passenger vessel of less than 100 gross tons is carrying more than six passengers for hire, it also may be seized. As another example, you might legally take eight friends fishing on your uninspected 26-foot flybridge cruiser, but not if one of them becomes a passenger for hire. An uninspected vessel is not an uncontrolled vessel. An uninspected vessel is subject to a boarding and safety inspection at any time, and if it exceeds the passenger limitations, it can be seized.

As has been shown, the types of passenger guidelines provide for both charter and passenger-for-hire revenues. In other words, you can treat a properly qualified vessel as a head boat or a party boat, use it as an excursion vessel or a bed-and-breakfast, turn it over to an agent, take out a charter party on it, or rent it to a charter party and wave as it sails into the sunset.

It is important to note that nowhere in the PVSA is the term "bareboat" used. Instead, the law makes a distinction in chartering based upon whether or not the boat is "chartered with the crew provided or specified by the owner or the owner's representative."

Prior to enactment of the PVSA, it was possible to bareboat charter uninspected vessels of virtually any size carrying large numbers of charter passengers. This is because no statute prevented the passenger charter industry from adapting the demise charter concepts used by the U.S. government in World War II for chartering merchant ships. However, in the industry today, three

Operation	*Vessel Type*
Not more than 6 passengers, 1 of whom is for hire, whether chartered or not.	Uninspected passenger vessel
More than 6 passengers, 1 of whom is for hire, whether chartered or not.	Small passenger vessel
Chartered with crew provided. Not more than 6 passengers.	Uninspected passenger vessel
Chartered with crew provided. More than 6 passengers.	Small passenger vessel
Chartered with no crew provided. Not more than 12 passengers.	Recreational vessel*
Chartered with no crew provided. More than 12 passengers.	Small passenger vessel
Submersible vessel, at least 1 passenger for hire.	Small passenger vessel
Not chartered, carrying any number of passengers. No passengers for hire.	Recreational vessel*

* A vessel is considered recreational only if it is not used to carry passengers for hire; not used as a charter vessel with crew provided; not used as a charter vessel with no crew provided carrying more than 12 passengers; and not used in other commercial services.

Fig. 9-1. Guidelines for operations: vessels under 100 gross tons

types of charters are clearly referenced: a charter with crew provided, a charter with no crew provided, and a demise charter for sailing schools (described below).

The industry uses the term bareboat to connote turning a boat over to a charter party without providing a captain or crew. The charter party might do its own provisioning, or the charter broker, charter company, or owner might do it. The boat is likely to be fully equipped with galley ware, bed clothing, and navigational charts. The charter party might even hire a captain and crew. The only thing "bare" about it is that it "has no crew provided or specified by the owner or the owner's representative." And it still must fit into one of the vessel types described.

DEMISE CHARTERS

These charters, authorized by the PVSA only for sailing schools, are restricted to certain large sailing vessels. A demise contract transfers complete possession, command, and control (PCC) of the vessel to the charter entity, generally for a

Operation	*Vessel Type*
Not more than 12 passengers, 1 of whom is for hire, whether chartered or not.	Uninspected passenger vessel
More than 12 passengers, 1 of whom is for hire, whether chartered or not.	Passenger vessel
Chartered with crew provided. Not more than 12 passengers.	Uninspected passenger vessel
Chartered with crew provided. More than 12 passengers.	Passenger vessel
Chartered with no crew provided. Not more than 12 passengers.	Recreational vessel*
Chartered with no crew provided. More than 12 passengers.	Passenger vessel
Submersible vessel, at least 1 passenger for hire.	Passenger vessel
Not chartered, carrying any number of passengers. No passengers for hire.	Recreational vessel*

* A vessel is considered recreational only if it is not used to carry passengers for hire; not used as a charter vessel with crew provided; not used as a charter vessel with no crew provided carrying more than 12 passengers; and not used in other commercial services.

Fig. 9-2. Guidelines for operations: vessels 100 gross tons or more

relatively long period of time. In essence, the charter entity becomes the true owner for that period. The charter generally requires three factors to be valid: (1) the contract must be valid, (2) the owner must indeed pass full PCC, and (3) the charter entity must accept and exercise full PCC.

SPECIAL INSPECTION PROVISIONS FOR CERTAIN VESSELS

The Coast Guard estimated that before enactment of the Passenger Vessel Safety Act of 1993 (PVSA), between five hundred and seven hundred uninspected yachts were carrying large numbers of passengers each by executing demise bareboat charters that were not illegal at that time. The PVSA prohibited this by essentially limiting the numbers of charter passengers on uninspected vessels to twelve. This meant that many uninspected party- and dinner-cruise boats and other yachts had to be certificated (inspected and issued certificates of inspection), if they were to carry legally more than the new minimums prescribed for uninspected vessels.

In order to ease the transition for these boats, many of which were of wooden or fiberglass construction, the act provided for special inspection provisions. Owners received an extension period of up to thirty months from June 20, 1994, in which to comply with the new provisions.

If you are a prospective purchaser of one of those vessels, you can ascertain which charter operations categorized in this chapter you may undertake, based upon whether the boat is still covered by a current extension letter, has received a certificate of inspection, or remains an uninspected vessel.

SUMMARY

Descriptive and graphical summaries of the regulations covered in this chapter follow. Note the distinction between *passengers* and *passengers for hire.*

1. A vessel of any tonnage that is not chartered and carries no passengers for hire may carry the number of passengers considered safe by the Coast Guard without the need for inspection. The number considered safe may be determined by observation or boarding by either Coast Guard or state marine patrols.
2. A vessel of less than 100 gross tons may carry one or more passengers for hire without the need for inspection as long as the combined number of passengers and passengers for hire would be no more than six.
3. A vessel of less than 100 gross tons that is chartered with crew provided or specified by the owner or the owner's representative may carry up to six passengers without the need for inspection.
4. A vessel of less than 100 gross tons that is chartered with no crew provided or specified by the owner or the owner's representative may carry up to twelve passengers without the need for inspection.
5. A vessel of at least 100 gross tons may carry one or more passengers for hire without the need for inspection as long as the combined number of passengers and passengers for hire would be no more than twelve.
6. A vessel of at least 100 gross tons that is chartered with the crew provided or specified by the owner or the owner's representative may carry up to twelve passengers without the need for inspection.
7. An inspected vessel that is chartered may carry the number of passengers and passengers for hire shown on its certificate of inspection.
8. Any submersible vessel that carries one or more passengers for hire must be inspected.
9. Figures 9-1 and 9-2 offer graphical summaries to assist in determining your boat's status. Note that figure 9-1 applies to vessels under 100 gross tons and figure 9-2 applies to vessels of 100 gross tons or more.

CHAPTER 10

Inspection and Certification

WHAT IS A VESSEL INSPECTION?

Inspection, for which the owner deals with the Coast Guard's inspection department, is a separate process from documentation. Inspection is *not* the same as a Coast Guard auxiliary courtesy inspection, or a Coast Guard boarding inspection. It is a detailed study that a Coast Guard marine inspection officer makes of the boat's construction and its passenger safety devices and facilities to ensure that they meet the written standards contained in Title 46 of the Code of Federal Regulations.[1]

Marine inspection officers operate from marine safety offices (MSO), marine inspection offices (MIO), marine safety detachments (MSD), and marine inspection detachments (MID). (Subsequent references in this chapter to these organizations are indicated by MSO/MIO.)

A charter boat owner involved in boat inspection should contact the MSO/MIO nearest to the boat's location. If the boat will be operating in an area outside the MSO/MIO's jurisdiction, the owner should also contact the appropriate MSO/MIO for that operating area. (For addresses of MSO/MIOs, see appendix I.)

If the inspection is satisfactory, the owner will receive a certificate of inspection (Coast Guard Form CG-841—Certificate of Inspection, or Coast Guard Form CG-3753—Certificate of Inspection for Small Passenger Vessels) that will describe the vessel, the route which she may travel, the minimum manning requirements, the major lifesaving equipment carried, the minimum fire extinguishing equipment and life preservers required to be carried, the maximum number of passengers and the maximum number of persons that may be carried, the name of the owner and operator, and any conditions of operations determined by the MSO/MIO. The period of validity is stated on the certificate.

The owner must place this certificate under glass or other transparent material in a prominent place on board, unless such posting would be impracticable. In such case, it must be kept on board to be shown on demand.

Along with the certificate of inspection, the owner receives a sticker showing that the boat has been inspected and the date the certificate expires. The sticker must be posted where passengers can see it when boarding.

WHICH VESSELS *MUST* BE INSPECTED?

When reading this section, keep in mind the differences between *passengers* and *passengers for hire* defined in chapter 9. Subject to the exceptions that follow, your vessel must be inspected if it:

- Measures less than 100 gross tons and you want to carry more than six passengers, including at least one passenger for hire;
- Measures less than 100 gross tons and you want to charter it with crew (provided or specified by you or your representative) to a charter party that will carry more than six passengers;
- Measures less than 100 gross tons and you want to charter it uncrewed to a charter party that will carry more than twelve passengers;
- Measures 100 gross tons or more and you want to carry more than twelve passengers, including at least one passenger for hire;
- Measures 100 gross tons or more and you want to charter it (with or without crew provided by you) to a charter party that will carry more than twelve passengers;
- Measures 15 gross tons or more and you want to carry cargo for hire;
- Is a submersible on which you want to carry one or more passengers for hire;
- Is a tank vessel or other larger, special-purpose vessel designated for inspection.

WHICH VESSELS ARE EXCEPTED?

A foreign-flagged vessel that does not engage in coastwise trade is not normally required to be inspected if its country of registry is a signatory of SOLAS (International Convention for Safety of Life at Sea). However, it is subject to verification that the country of registry has carried out an inspection. Also excepted from the inspection requirements are boats that operate exclusively upon waters that have been declared nonnavigable. (For more on nonnavigable waters, see section on "Navigable Waters of the United States" in chapter 8.)

PASSENGER CAPACITIES FOR INSPECTED VESSELS

Regulations of progressive complexity divide the passenger fleet into three categories. These categories may be referred to as "T" boats, "K" boats, and "H" vessels. Each term derives from the subchapter in 46 CFR that regulates that type of vessel. (Subchapter K was being prepared by federal agencies as this book was going to the printer.)

The small passenger vessels and passenger vessels discussed below are the same inspected vessels discussed in chapter 9. A charter operator, as the term is used in this book, may use any of these boats in accordance with the guidelines in that chapter when they are properly certified and manned (for manning, see chapter 11).

Subchapter T-Boats

Small passenger vessels regulated by Subchapter T are vessels measuring less than 100 gross tons that do not exceed 200 feet in length. T-boats may be certified to carry 150 or fewer passengers, or 49 or fewer overnight passengers.

Subchapter K-Boats

Small passenger vessels regulated by Subchapter K also measure less than 100 gross tons and do not exceed 200 feet in length. However they are designated for inspection as K-boats to identify that they may be certified for an increased passenger capacity of 151 to 600, or an overnight capacity of 50 to 150.

Section K1-Boats

Within Subchapter K is a K1 section for a small number of existing small passenger vessels that measure less than 100 gross tons but are 200 feet or more in length. These boats may be certified for more than 600 passengers or more than 150 overnight passengers.

Subchapter H-Vessels

Passenger vessels regulated by Subchapter H are vessels measuring 100 gross tons or more. A passenger vessel may be certified for the number of passengers or overnight passengers that the marine inspection officer deems suitable for that particular vessel.

HOW TO GET A CERTIFICATE OF INSPECTION

Listed below are seven ways to get your certificate of inspection.

1. Buy a new boat with the certificate of inspection affixed in your name. This can be relatively simple, depending upon the type of charter operation you are considering. Just leaf through the advertising in boating or maritime magazines that are slanted toward the type of chartering operation you are contemplating. As part of the deal, the builder normally guarantees a certificated boat.
2. Buy a used boat that has already been inspected. Before you close the deal, you can apply for a renewal certificate, thus making sure the vessel still fits the Coast Guard criteria. Be aware, however, that if the boat is certified within the jurisdiction of an MSO/MIO different from yours, the inspection must be transferred to yours.
3. Order a sister ship to a boat that has already been certified. You will avoid going over new ground with the MSO/MIO, and it also might mean that the office already has acceptable plans.
4. Check out a listing of the inspected boats your nearest MSO/MIO controls, find one you like, *then* find a sister ship for sale.
5. Build your own boat similar to an existing certified boat.
6. Build a new model to fit your chartering needs. An example of success is Captain Mike Bomar, of Capt. Mike's Watersports in St. Pete Beach, Florida. Doing the work themselves, he and an associate built a 36-foot fiberglass catamaran parasail platform "from the bottom up, by following CFR references and coordinating closely with the Coast Guard."[2] Captain Mike reports that he drew up plans from a catamaran sailboat and cleared them with the Coast Guard. The Coast Guard made inspections and conducted stability and hull strength tests at specified percentages of completion. After certificating the boat, Bomar built a second one, and told me he is prepared to build others on contract. His vessels are certified for thirty-eight passengers each.
7. Convert a boat. This can be a costly project if not planned and carried out carefully. For instance, adding rails around your decks alone might mean a major modification of gunwale, decking, and hull. Then there might be retrofits involving rewiring, installation of collision bulkheads, new plumbing, and a dozen or more other projects. A few dollars from consultants on the front end might save you thousands later. So get the best possible advice from experts, such as naval architects and builders, and turn the MSO/MIO into your second home. For ideas about what such a project entails, see appendix E.

Once you have located a boat or have decided to build one, contact the MSO/MIO nearest to the boat's location. If the boat will operate in *another*

MSO/MIO jurisdiction, contact that organization also. Prior to the start of construction (or before the initial inspection, if it is a used boat), the MSO/MIO will need detailed copies of the plans. The marine inspector will tell you exactly what is needed and probably will provide information on how to prepare your input. This brings me to the best advice I've ever heard about how to get a certificate of inspection. It came from a chief bos'n's mate who said, "Just find out what the old %@$& wants and give it to him."

Any boat used to carry passengers or cargo for hire that is not required to be inspected earns the title "uninspected vessel." This does not exclude it, however, from the watchful eyes of the Coast Guard. Uninspected vessels have their own sets of regulations, such as maximum passenger loads and required safety equipment. The Coast Guard enforces safety regulations for uninspected vessels by courtesy inspections, random boardings, and boardings as a result of casualty.

SUMMARY

1. When estimating profitability of an inspected vessel for your chartering business, you should consider whether it will be regulated by Subchapter T, K (including Section K-1), or H of 46 CFR.
2. When contemplating inspection, you must consider the vessel size, the number of passengers you wish to carry, and whether you intend to charter.
3. Any boat carrying passengers or cargo for hire that is not required to be inspected is regulated under the rules for uninspected vessels.
4. Doing careful homework before starting the inspection procedure can save time and money.
5. When preparing for an inspection, find out everything the MSO/MIO wants and accomplish it.
6. Appendix D gives a summary of what it might take to convert a pleasure boat for certification.

CHAPTER 11

Captains' Licenses, Certificates, and Endorsements

IMPLICATIONS OF STATE OPERATOR LICENSING LAWS

Members of the National Association of State Boating Law Administrators have approved a model act for state vessel operator licensing. In April 1994, Alabama became the first state to enact such a law. Other states are expected to follow. Exceptions listed in the model act were some nonresidents and operators of rented or chartered vessels. Also excepted were those who possess a valid master's, mate's, or operator's license issued by the Coast Guard. It appears that if you must have a Coast Guard license for your charter business, you won't need a state operator's license.

WHO MUST HAVE A COAST GUARD LICENSE?

In general, anybody operating a boat on navigable waters will need a license to:[1]

- Carry one or more passengers for hire;
- Carry one or more charter passengers when he or she is the owner or representative of the owner;
- Carry one or more charter passengers for a consideration;
- Carry cargo for hire;
- Operate any inspected vessel.

Information in this chapter was obtained from the Passenger Vessel Safety Act of 1993 *(codified in 46 U.S.C.); and 46 CFR Subchapter B, Part 10:* Licensing of Maritime Personnel.

What Is a Passenger for Hire?

Chapter 9 explains that passengers for hire are passengers that have paid a *consideration* to the owner or the owner's agent. To be carrying passengers for hire, you don't have to stand at the boarding ladder collecting tickets. If consideration is contributed at any phase of your chartering business, and the customer takes a ride on your boat, the captain needs to be licensed.

The definition of consideration allows an exception when you take one or more friends out who help defray expenses of the outing. For instance, a person who goes fishing with the owner/skipper and voluntarily pays for food, drink, or bait is not paying a consideration. In addition, when an employer takes employees out for fun or entertainment, or takes clients or business associates out for entertainment, it is not necessarily a "for hire" situation.[2] However, charter operators who try to bend this exception to fit their business can find themselves paying as much as a $25,000 fine. Consider the examples that follow.

Six people pay Joe Divemaster to teach them how to dive. He explains that his fee covers the classroom and swimming pool sessions. As a "bonus," or "discount," he will transport them "free" to their end-of-course open-water dive sites by barge, at no charge. The open-water site is in a protected cove of a river less than 500 yards from shore. Nevertheless, the Coast Guard says he needs a license because he is on navigable waters and is receiving a consideration.

A student signs up with a school to learn to sail on a boat equipped with an auxiliary. During the practical application periods, her teacher—who is employed by the school as a classroom instructor—accompanies her. The instructor's contract with the school forbids him from touching the rigging or the helm. Never mind—whether or not he touches the rigging or the helm, he is carrying a passenger for hire. The sailing-school owner who learned this the hard way paid thousands of dollars by the time his court sessions were over.

Ski boats need licensed operators to tow customers in navigable waters—which means along saltwater beaches, in rivers, or on most streams and lakes. So do parasail boats and boats that tow or launch hang gliders. Also, if customers are ferried to or lifted from a parasail barge or a hang glider barge, the ferry operator and the barge operator must be licensed. (And if the ferry operator takes a second group of six passengers to the barge without returning the first six, the barge must be inspected.) The same rules apply to fishing guides and hunting guides, harbor excursion-vessel operators, airboat tour guides, and glass-bottomed boat operators.

The requirement holds whether a boat is under way or at anchor. For example, a commercial dive-boat operator with divers in the water must keep a licensed operator on board at all times. If the boat is anchored and the skipper wants to attend the dive, he'd better leave another licensed operator on board.

Why the latter requirement? The answer is twofold. First, the regulations require that the operator of a boat carrying passengers for hire be licensed. This is a means of creating a minimum level of safety protection for the passengers. Second, even though the passengers may be diving, a licensed operator on board assures that there will be a safe boat for their return. The operator can monitor the weather, take steps to prevent or stop dragging, discover and suppress fire or flooding, and do all the other things that would be done for safety when the passengers are aboard.

If you believe you have a watertight plan to avoid obtaining a captain's license, you might get an opinion about it from the Coast Guard. Your plan might fit within the law, but you are in business to make profits, and the bottom line suffers when the overhead rises, whether it be from debt service or legal costs. So be careful about tying your operation into a legal knot that might fall off and foul your prop just when you're well under way. If your plan could cost you more money in the courts than it is likely to return in profits, it might be simpler to get a license or hire employees with licenses.

How Do the Laws Apply in Foreign Countries?

The United States recognizes equivalent licenses issued by countries that are members of SOLAS (International Convention of Safety of Life at Sea) that provide reciprocity. However, if the boat is flagged in the United States and is to be used commercially anywhere in the world, the owner must comply with U.S. law regarding inspection, documentation, and licensing. If it is U.S. documented, the operator in most cases must be a U.S. citizen. If it is state numbered, the operator may be a noncitizen, but must have an equivalent foreign license that is recognized by the United States. If it carries more than six passengers for hire, it must have a valid certificate of inspection, and the operator must be licensed accordingly. If the vessel carries commercial cargo, such as cheese, up and down the Meuse River in Holland, the vessel must be under control of a Coast Guard licensed operator.

TONNAGE LIMITATIONS

This section and the section on route restrictions that follows cover the operator, master, and mate licenses commonly required to carry passengers. Those licenses are listed below. Excluded are licenses above 200 gross tons, engineer licenses, and licenses for special purpose vessels, such as commercial fishing vessels, towing vessels, and vessels used in the offshore oil industry. Information for those licenses can be found in other reference materials.[3]

- Operator of (small) Uninspected Passenger Vessels, under 100 Gross Tons (OUPV, or "Six-Pack")
- Master—Not More Than 100 Gross Tons
- Master/Mate—Not More Than 200 Gross Tons

The OUPV or "six-pack" license restricts the operator to uninspected vessels of under 100 gross tons. In order to operate any vessel other than an OUPV, the captain must have a license of sufficient tonnage for the vessel. A master (100 tons) may serve as an OUPV within the route restrictions of the license, regardless of the tonnage restriction on the license. A master (200 tons) may operate a vessel of lesser tonnage, including an OUPV vessel within the route restrictions of the license. A mate is authorized in some instances to operate a vessel of less tonnage than that of the mate's license. However, a mate may operate a vessel within the tonnage limitation of the license only when a properly licensed master is aboard or available.

Actual tonnage limitations for the licenses for 100 gross tons and 200 gross tons are determined in 50-ton increments, based upon the tonnage of the vessels used for qualifying time. However, if all the qualifying service was on a vessel or vessels of 5 gross tons or less, the license will be issued for 25 gross tons. Thus, a person might have a "100-ton" or "200-ton" license that authorizes operation only as master of vessels of lesser tonnage.

Tonnage limits can be raised by serving additional qualifying time on larger vessels and by meeting the additional requirements for the higher tonnage, such as radar observer qualification, fire-fighting training, service as an able seaman, and an additional exam.

ROUTE RESTRICTIONS

In addition to gross tonnage limitations, licenses carry one of the route restrictions listed below to indicate the waters on which the holder is allowed to serve. These restrictions stem from the waters upon which the applicant served qualifying time.

Specific Area. Allows service only on waters specified by the Coast Guard licensing office. A limited license is issued for a specific area.

Western Rivers. Allows service on the waters of the Mississippi River and its tributaries, as outlined in 46 CFR 10.103.

Great Lakes. Allows service on the Great Lakes and their connecting and tributary waters, as defined in 46 CFR 10.103.

Inland. Allows service on all waters (except the Great Lakes) inside the *boundary line*, as described in 46 CFR Part 7. The boundary line generally follows the trend of the shoreline and jumps directly across entrances to bays, inlets, and rivers, i.e., jetty to jetty. However, along the Gulf Coast, the boundary line extends up to 12 miles offshore.

Because some "inland" areas include waters covered by the international rules of the road, an applicant for an inland license will be tested on the International Rules as well as the Inland Rules of the Road. An exception to this requirement for the International Rules is authorized when applying for a license restricted to "inland waters, excluding those waters covered by the COLREGS" (International Rules of the Road).

A Great Lakes endorsement may be obtained for an inland license after ninety days of Great Lakes service.

Near Coastal. Allows service on waters within 200 miles off any coastline around the world and on inland waters. An exception is the OUPV, limited to 100 miles offshore.

Oceans. No limitation anywhere in the world.

Route restrictions can be enlarged through qualifying time in new routes and by meeting the additional requirements to qualify for the license. For example, to upgrade an inland license to a near coastal license would require an exam on the International Rules of the Road (if not previously given) and the specified number of days of qualifying time on near coastal waters. (Near coastal waters are waters seaward of the COLREGS demarcation line, marking where the International Rules of the Road apply.)

LICENSES FOR RIVERS

Licenses also are available for routes limited to rivers, which are defined as "any river, canal, or other similar body of water designated by the Officer in Charge, Marine Inspection."[4] Service requirements remain the same as for Great Lakes and inland licenses, but the plotting portion of the exam for a Great Lakes or inland license is replaced with a requirement to demonstrate proficiency in navigational instruments and chart skills which are necessary in river service.

OTHER LIMITED LICENSES

Under the regulations, a fishing or hunting guide who uses a boat on navigable waters while working needs a license. Let's say that Joe Fishmaster operates a bass boat on an inland lake near his home. Must he know everything a skipper should know who takes a six-pack boat up and down the eastern seaboard for sport fishing? No. He may qualify for a limited license.

Limited OUPV and master (not more than 100 gross tons) licenses with Great Lakes (GL), inland (IN), rivers (RI), and near-coastal (NC) restrictions are also authorized for yacht clubs, formal camps, educational institutions, and marinas.[5]

Applicants for limited master licenses with four months' operating experience, and applicants for limited OUPV licenses with three months' experience, are eligible for a limited examination if they have satisfactorily completed a boating course approved by the National Association of State Boating Law Administrators, a public education course conducted by the U.S. Power Squadron or the American Red Cross, or a Coast Guard–approved course. They may be excused from the first aid and cardiopulmonary resuscitation (CPR) requirements, depending upon judgment of the officer in charge of marine inspection concerning availability of medical assistance.

BASIC REQUIREMENTS FOR ALL LICENSES

Fourteen basic requirements must be met in order to attain any OUPV, master, or mate license described in this chapter.

1. Minimum age. Based upon type of license.
2. Qualifying time. You must have a minimum amount of experience on the water, based upon type of license. Although most of this can be accumulated during a lifetime, at least ninety days must have been in the last thirty-six months. For the larger licenses, certain amounts of qualifying time must be on vessels of specified sizes. Note that 46 CFR counts a year as 360 days, six months as 180 days, and three months as 90 days.

   Qualifying time may be on pleasure boats, with eight hours counting as a day. Some regional exam centers (RECs) allow four hours to count as a day on vessels under 100 gross tons. On commercial boats, eight hours may count as a day, but if you stand twelve-hour watches, each watch counts as a day and a half. Policies can vary from one REC to another (see appendix I for addresses of RECs). Check with either the nearest REC or a knowledgeable license prep organization.

   Time employed in deck service counts, time aboard an uncrewed charter boat counts, and time aboard a crewed charter boat may count also—if the owner or skipper certifies that you were helping to operate the boat as a crew member. Living aboard—at a pier, on a mooring, or at anchor—does not normally count as qualifying time. Nor does time as a paying, nonworking passenger aboard a dive-boat, a head boat, a party boat, or any other vessel count.

If your qualifying day on the water takes you across the COLREGS demarcation line (marking where the International Rules of the Road apply), that day counts as a qualifying day on ocean or near-coastal waters.

If you are an owner of a boat under 200 gross tons, you can attest to your own service on that boat. If your qualifying time is noncommercial on somebody else's boat, a letter from the owner is normally required, although the REC might accept a letter from a marina operator or anybody else qualified to know. If your time is commercial, you will need letters, discharges, or other acceptable documents from owners or licensed persons. For sea service as a member of the armed forces, you will need an official transcript.

The Coast Guard has approved some training courses, including simulator training, that might be acceptable for part of the qualifying time. The nearest REC can advise further on this.

3. Physical exam. Your physician, or physician's assistant, must certify the following in writing, which can be done on a standard Coast Guard form (CG-719K): (a) that your general physical condition does not indicate epilepsy, insanity, senility, acute general disease or neurosyphilis, badly impaired hearing, or any other defect that would render you incompetent to perform the ordinary duties that your license would entail; (b) that you have uncorrected vision of at least 20/200 in each eye correctable to at least 20/40 in each eye; and (c) that your color sense is satisfactory when tested by any of the following: Pseudo-isochromatic Plates, Eldridge Green Color Perception Lantern, Farnsworth Lantern, Keystone Orthoscope, Keystone Tele-binocular, SAMCTT, Titmus Optical Vision Tester, or Williams Lantern.

   If a physical deficiency exists, the case can be sent to the commandant of the Coast Guard for a second opinion. The key here is first to convince the officer in charge, marine inspection (OCMI), that extenuating circumstances exist. Recommendations from owners and skippers concerning your proven abilities can help. Even color blindness is not an absolute bar to a license, because it is possible to obtain a license restricted to daytime use.

4. Proof of U.S. citizenship. U.S. citizenship is required to command any vessel other than an uninspected, undocumented vessel, except for certain inspected vessels in the U.S. Virgin Islands.
5. English. You must be able to speak and understand English (exceptions available for Puerto Rico).

6. First aid. You should have completed a first aid course within the previous twelve months from the American National Red Cross, a Coast Guard–approved school, or a school the OCMI determines exceeds the standards of the Red Cross course.
7. CPR. You should possess a currently valid certificate of completion of a CPR course from the American National Red Cross, the American Heart Association, or a Coast Guard–approved school.
8. Character references. Obtain recommendations from three persons who have knowledge of your suitability for duty. If your qualifying time derives from pleasure cruises, the recommendations can be from anybody who knows you. If your qualifying time is commercial, the recommendations must be from licensed officers, one of whom must be a master.
9. You must have no recent narcotics violations and must not have been convicted of a violation of the narcotic drug laws of the United States, the District of Columbia, or any state or territory of the United States, within three years prior to the date of filing the application (ten years if the gravity of the facts or circumstances warrant).
10. You must have no drug addiction and must never have been the user of or addicted to the use of a narcotic drug, unless you furnish satisfactory evidence that you are "cured."
11. You must pass a drug test.
12. Fingerprints. Submit fingerprint forms provided by the REC at time of application. These will be sent to the FBI. If through fingerprinting or any other source the OCMI receives information indicating that your lifestyle and character suggest that you cannot be entrusted with the duties and responsibilities of the license you are applying for, your application may be rejected. You may appeal such rejection.
13. Driving and criminal records. Since January 18, 1996, the Coast Guard has been authorized to check the National Driver Register and to review criminal records for cases of conviction of serious crimes and certain motor vehicle offenses. License applications will not be approved during an assessment period specified for each offense. If you have been convicted of a serious offense, check with the REC or a license prep school for further information.
14. Written exam. Either a comprehensive or limited exam is required for all licenses. Comprehensive exams are covered in detail in a later section.

REQUIREMENTS FOR SPECIFIC LICENSES[6]

These abbreviations pertaining to route restrictions previously discussed apply: Great Lakes = GL, Inland = IN, Rivers = RI, Near Coastal = NC, and Oceans = OC.

Operator of Uninspected (Small) Passenger Vessels, Less Than 100 Gross Tons (OUPV) (GL/IN/RI/NC)

Within route restrictions, an OUPV (also called a six-pack licensee) may carry from one to six passengers for hire, so long as the total number of passengers and passengers for hire does not exceed six (see definitions in chapter 9). If the boat is chartered, an OUPV provided by the owner may carry up to six charter passengers.

Because the license applies to vessels with any type of propulsion machinery, it includes sailboats with auxiliary engines or motors. (Uninspected sailboats of less than 100 tons with *no* auxiliary power do not require the operators to be licensed.)

An OUPV cannot legally operate an inspected vessel, even if it is carrying six or fewer passengers for hire and/or passengers. Neither can an OUPV operate an uninspected vessel of 100 gross tons or more.

The OUPV license is the only U.S. license a non-U.S. citizen can hold. If issued to a noncitizen, it will be limited on its face to undocumented vessels.

The requirements (in addition to requirements for *all* licenses) are:

1. The minimum age is eighteen.
2. Qualifying time is 360 days. For the near-coastal endorsement (not more than 100 miles offshore for six-pack operators), at least 90 days must be on ocean or near-coastal waters. For Great Lakes authority, qualifying time must include at least 90 days on the lakes.
3. All applicants must be able to speak, read, and understand English, except for Spanish-speaking applicants who intend to operate in the vicinity of Puerto Rico, who may apply for a license restricted to that area.
4. A comprehensive exam is required.

Master, Not More Than 100 Gross Tons (GL/IN/RI/NC)

A "Master 100 GT (GL/IN/RI/NC)" may command an inspected vessel within the route and tonnage limitations of the license. He or she may also serve as an OUPV within the route restrictions (but not the tonnage limitations) of the license. Requirements (in addition to requirements for *all* licenses) are:

1. The minimum age is nineteen.
2. Qualifying time (IN/RI) is 360 days of service on any waters. Great Lakes authority requires at least 90 days of that service on the lakes.
3. Qualifying time (NC) is 720 days of deck service, at least 360 days of which must have been on ocean or near-coastal routes.
4. For a sail or auxiliary sail endorsement, an applicant (GL/IN/RI) must have served 180 days at any time aboard the respective type of vessel. An applicant (NC) must have served 360 days.
5. A comprehensive exam is required.

Master/Mate, Not More Than 200 Gross Tons (GL/IN/RI)

A "Master 200 GT (GL/IN/RI)" may command an inspected vessel within the route and tonnage limitations of the license. He or she also may serve as OUPV within the route restrictions (but not the tonnage limitations) of the license. He or she may command uninspected vessels of 100 gross tons or greater within the route and tonnage limits on the license.

A "Mate 200 GT (GL/IN/RI)" may serve as mate within the route and tonnage limitations of the license. He or she may not command any vessel other than to stand watches when a licensed master or captain is aboard. Requirements (in addition to the requirements for *all* licenses) are:

1. The minimum age is nineteen for master; eighteen for mate.
2. For master, qualifying time is 360 days of service on vessels, 180 days of which must have been as master, mate, or equivalent supervisory position while holding a license as master, mate, operator, or second-class operator of uninspected towing vessels, or OUPV. Great Lakes authority requires at least 90 days of qualifying time on the lakes.
3. For mate, qualifying time is 180 days of service in the deck department of steam, motor, sail, or auxiliary sail vessels.
4. For a sail or auxiliary sail endorsement, a master must have served 180 days at any time aboard the respective type vessel. A mate must have served 90 days.
5. An exam is required.

Master/Mate, Not More Than 200 Gross Tons (OC/NC)

A "Master 200 GT (OC/NC)" may command an inspected vessel within the route and tonnage limitations of the license. He or she also may serve as OUPV within the route restrictions (but not the tonnage limitations) of the license. He or she may command uninspected vessels of 100 gross tons or greater within the route and tonnage limits on the license.

A "Mate 200 GT (NC)" may serve as a mate on an inspected vessel within the route and tonnage limitations of the license. He or she also may serve as OUPV within the route restrictions (but not the tonnage limitations) of the license. Requirements (in addition to the requirements for *all* licenses) are:

1. The minimum ages are twenty-one for master (OC), nineteen for master (NC), and eighteen for mate (NC). (There is no license for mate [OC], 200 gross tons.)
2. Qualifying time for master (OC) is (a) 1,080 days of service on ocean or near-coastal waters, including at least 720 days as a licensed master mate, or equivalent supervisory position, while holding a license as master, mate, or OUPV. Service on inland waters may substitute for a maximum of 540 of the required three years; or (b) 720 days of service as a licensed operator or second-class operator of uninspected towing vessels upon ocean or near-coastal waters, and completion of a limited examination.
3. In addition to the qualifying time, an applicant for master (OC) must have certificates for able seaman (AB), fire fighting, and radar observer. The AB is earned by serving as an able seaman and passing an exam. Fire-fighting and radar observer certificates are earned by attending Coast Guard–approved courses.
4. Qualifying time for master (NC) is 720 days service, of which at least 360 days must have been as master, mate, or equivalent supervisory position while holding a license as master, mate, or OUPV. At least 360 days of the qualifying time must have been on ocean or near-coastal waters; or 360 days as licensed operator or second-class operator of ocean or near-coastal uninspected towing vessels, and completion of a limited examination.
5. Qualifying time for mate (NC) is 360 days of service in the deck department on vessels of any propulsion, at least 180 days of which must have been in ocean or near-coastal waters; or 90 days of service in the deck department of steam or motor vessels operating on ocean, near-coastal, Great Lakes, or inland waters while holding a license as

master of Great Lakes and inland steam or motor, sail, or auxiliary sail-propelled vessels of not more than 200 gross tons; or the holder of an OUPV license with a near-coastal route endorsement who completes a limited examination.

6. For a sail or auxiliary sail endorsement, a master must have served 360 days at any time aboard the respective type vessel, and a mate must have served 180 days; or a master of steam or motor vessels with 90 days of service aboard a sail or auxiliary sail vessel may get an endorsement for the respective type of vessel.
7. An exam is required for each license.

THE WRITTEN EXAM

Ultimately, the Coast Guard wants every candidate for a license to receive skills training. In its 1993 report, "Licensing 2000 and Beyond," the agency forecasts moving toward such competency training. However, in the interim, most applicants are still being approved for licensing on the basis of minimum service periods on the water, coupled with a comprehensive written exam.

The written exam is multiple choice. Although there is no time limit, it must be completed in one sitting. Most applicants finish within four to six hours. If you finish early, it is wise to review every question and check every calculation.

The questions are not supposed to be misleading, but they *can* be difficult. The section on the rules of the road is the most exacting, because the Coast Guard sets 90 percent as a passing grade for this section, which is a closed-book session. A grade of 70 percent will do for the other three sections: plotting, seamanship, and safety.

Plotting is fairly straightforward for an experienced coastwise pilot, but a high-tech skipper who relies exclusively on loran and GPS may have to do some catch-up study. If you can plot a course, convert from magnetic to true courses, work set-and-drift problems, do tide and current calculations, and read the notes on a chart, you will be in good shape. Although the Coast Guard provides instruments, you might be more comfortable bringing your own parallel rulers, nautical slide rule, and dividers. And a nonprogrammable calculator can be helpful.

Information about the questions on seamanship and safety will be found in the references listed in this chapter. Some of these references will be available during the exam (except during the section on the rules of the road), so the more familiar you are with them, the more helpful they will be.

The Coast Guard estimates that ten thousand people take basic exams each year—and only 60 percent pass. You must pass every section to get your license. If you fail one or two sections, you can retake them—twice within the following three months. If you haven't passed all sections by then, you will be required to wait three months before trying again and will have to take the entire examination at that time. If you fail three or more sections, you will have to take and pass a complete reexamination. If you fail three or more sections the second time, you will be required to wait (i.e., study) three months before trying again.

Studying the References

Applicants with a broad base of marine experience and a fairly good educational background often succeed with this method of preparation. You should be able to schedule study periods and stick to the schedule. You will need to create a study program for yourself, just as a teacher creates a syllabus for students. You should match the reference materials against the subjects the Coast Guard expects you to know (see appendix C), organize each subject into logical components, develop learning aids for retention, and discover your weaknesses and find ways to overcome them. If you have already taken a U.S. Power Squadron course or a Coast Guard Auxiliary course, you'll have a leg up. If you haven't, you probably will want to concentrate strictly on your study program. This method of preparation can cost less than the other two methods if you already have the reference materials or can borrow them. Here are examples of references you might need (see bibliography for full reference):

- *Chapman Piloting, Seamanship and Small Boat Handling*
- Bowditch: *American Practical Navigator*
- *The Ship's Medicine Chest and First Aid at Sea*
- *Light List, List of Lights, Radio Navigational Aids, Coast Pilot, Sailing Directions, Tide Tables, Tidal Current Tables, and Nautical Chart No. 1*
- Koch: *Weather for the Mariner*
- Maritime Administration: *Marine Fire Prevention, Firefighting, and Fire Safety*
- IALA buoyage system pamphlet
- *Watchkeeping for Seafarers* (STCW), 1978
- *International Regulations for Preventing Collisions at Sea*, 1972, and Inland Navigation Rules (Rules of the Road)
- U.S. Code of Federal Regulations: Title 33 and Volumes 1 and 2 of Title 46

If you know *everything* in the references, you will be as savvy as Captain Horatio Hornblower. But the scope of information in *Chapman* or Bowditch alone can be formidable, and often peripheral to the mission at hand, which is to answer correctly the specific questions on the exam.

You must be able to convert your knowledge into answers that the Coast Guard will accept. For some questions, two possible choices might seem equally correct. For others *no* answer looks right. This is why even Horatio Hornblower might opt for either a home-study prep course or a class at a license prep school.

Home-Study Prep Courses

A home-study prep course generally requires the same background and abilities that you need for studying the references. Additionally, although a home-study course can create the study program for you, you will still have to schedule your own study periods and stick to the schedule.

The course might be nothing more than a study manual, a course outline, and a large number of sample questions and answers. Or it might include additional texts, as well as computer disks and videotapes, which will increase the cost, but will enhance learning.

Sample questions and answers quickly help you find your weaknesses while reinforcing learning points and getting you used to the mechanics of the exam. However, avoid a tendency to memorize questions. With the addition or deletion of just one word, two similar looking questions might need completely different answers.

Do some questions really vary by just a word or two? Definitely. The Coast Guard keeps a thirty thousand–question database covering each subject in the exam. To prepare a specific test, they randomly select a percentage of questions from each of those subjects. Thus, today's question might read one way, while tomorrow's might read entirely the opposite. This makes it important to learn—even memorize—principles, and the way they are presented in questions, but not the questions themselves.

License Prep Schools

Home study is not for everyone. Many charter-boat captains will swear that they never could have obtained their licenses without first attending a license prep school. The trade-off for classroom instruction is cost. This is generally the most expensive method of preparing for the exam.

A prep school can do just about everything except take the exam for you. The school creates the study program, schedules your study time and makes you stick to the schedule, and might even guarantee your money back if you don't pass the exam.

The instructor will teach the principles, go over sample questions, and use practice tests. The instructor can also clarify points that might be indecipherable at home, help with applications and qualification forms, and steer you past bureaucratic roadblocks that sometimes tend to obscure the destination—taking and passing the exam.

Courses generally last from seven to ten days or evenings. Some schools offer weekend courses for applicants who have enough background to assimilate the material in two days. Some schools tailor their programs to the student's schedule. In any case, think in terms of about forty hours to go through this compressed form of preparation.

Some prep school organizations do not provide all the services described, or at most merely give them lip service. Shop around, and talk to the captains who know. If you select this third method of preparation, invest your money where you will get the service you need.

Which method of preparation is best for you? Make a careful appraisal of what you know and *don't* know. Assess your chances of success with each method. Talk to a captain who had your level of knowledge when he or she took the exam. How many times did it take to pass? Decide how much time and money you are willing to spend in preparation; then make your selection.

Arranging to Take the Exam

If you take a license prep course, the instructor can tell you where and when the exams are given in your area. Otherwise, contact the nearest REC (see appendix I). One REC might interpret portions of the Coast Guard regulations differently from another, so if you have an unusual situation and need a second opinion, you might try another REC. Bear in mind that you are prohibited from formally applying at more than one REC at the same time.

If you are living overseas, you may be able to take the exam without returning to the United States. Contact U.S. Coast Guard Headquarters, 2100 2nd Street SW, Washington, D.C. 20593, to ascertain which office handles your country of residence.

LICENSE RENEWALS

All licenses expire at the end of five years. Unlike most state driver's license agencies, the Coast Guard doesn't send notices of license expirations. However, it does allow for leeway. First, you can renew up to twelve months in advance. And, should you forget, you can renew up to twelve months after the license has expired. Be careful of the latter; you can't legally operate with the license during the grace period. Even if more than twelve months have passed since the expiration date, mitigating circumstances may save the day. If you have an unusual case, check with the OCMI.

Another option is to make your license inactive by renewing it "for continuity." When renewed for continuity, you cannot use the license, but you can activate it at any time by fulfilling the requirements for renewal (below), and *without* having to take the full exam again. To renew for continuity, your application for renewal has to include the license (or a copy), and a signed statement that you are aware of the restrictions that will be placed on the license and the requirements for rescinding the continuity endorsement before you may activate your license and use it again. The requirements for renewal of any license are as follows:

1. Present evidence of at least one year of sea service (or acceptable substitute) during the past five years; pass a comprehensive, open-book exercise; complete an approved refresher training course; or present evidence of closely related employment for three of the past five years and demonstrate knowledge by taking an applicable Rules of the Road exercise.
2. Obtain a medical certification from a licensed physician or physician's assistant, including a report of visual acuity and hearing. For renewals, if an applicant has lost the sight of one eye, this does *not* disqualify, if the vision in the remaining eye is 20/400 uncorrected and 20/40 corrected.
3. Successfully pass a drug urinalysis test at an approved laboratory.

To renew your license, go to the nearest REC (see appendix I) or renew by mail. Send the following to the REC that issued the license:

1. Application on a Coast Guard–furnished form.
2. The license to be renewed, or a photocopy if it has not yet expired.
3. The medical and drug certification previously described.
4. Evidence of the required sea service or an acceptable substitute, the refresher training, or the closely related employment.
5. If renewing for continuity, the statement (previously described) that you are aware of the restrictions and the requirements for reactivating.

In the absence of sea service or any of the alternatives, the open-book exercise may be administered through the mail.

LICENSING COSTS

First aid and CPR certification are often available from the Red Cross or county emergency medical sources for fees starting at around $50. These costs likely should not be considered as part of licensing, because anybody using boats needs to be current in both areas.

Home-study prep courses start at about $40 (for a question-and-answer book or disk), and classroom courses begin at about $350. An estimate for what you might want to spend in order to get a good guarantee would be $200 and $500, respectively.

Physical exams and drug screenings are available in many locations for about $75. The names of approved screening laboratories can be obtained from the REC or a license prep school. Many prep schools will bring qualified individuals on site to administer physicals between class sessions.

Coast Guard user fees for first-time licensing will run just under $200 in increments. First is evaluation and the FBI check, for $82. If you are unsure about your qualifications, you might obtain an informal reading from a major license prep organization before paying the evaluation charge to the Coast Guard. Next comes the exam, for $80. Be sure to pass the first time, because you will have to pay another exam fee each time you are reexamined. Once you pass the exam, the charge for issuing the license will be $35.

MERCHANT MARINER'S DOCUMENTS

Each crew member (including licensed personnel) serving on merchant vessels over 100 gross tons operating offshore or on the Great Lakes must hold a merchant mariner's document (MMD). These documents, issued by the Coast Guard, are often called "Z-cards" in the industry. Exemptions include barges, fishing or whaling vessels, sail-school instructors and students, and scientific personnel on oceanographic research vessels.

Entry-level MMDs, with neither sea time nor written examination required, are endorsed to cover the three departments on a ship—deck, engine, and steward. Experience and other prerequisites authorize an MMD-holder to progress to qualified ratings. Entry-level MMDs are:

- Ordinary Seaman/Wiper—Authorizes the holder to work in either the deck or the engine department.
- Food Handler—Authorizes service in the steward's department (requires a physical exam).

CERTIFICATES OF REGISTRY

U.S. law provides for the issuance of certificates of registry to certain officers who perform nonmaritime functions on specified vessels operating on offshore or Great Lakes waters. Although the Coast Guard gives no exam, these certificates require varying types of service and other qualifications, including U.S.

citizenship. Certificates may be issued for pursers, medical doctors, professional nurses, marine physician's assistants, and hospital corpsmen.

SUMMARY

1. Anybody who operates a boat on navigable waters and carries a passenger for hire or a charter passenger needs a license from the Coast Guard. The type of license required depends upon whether the boat is inspected or uninspected, in what waters it will be operated, and its gross tonnage.
2. The hierarchy is as follows: An OUPV (six-pack operator) may command an uninspected vessel of less than 100 gross tons within route limitations. A mate, 100 or 200 gross tons, may serve under a master on a vessel within the tonnage and route limitations common to both officers. When serving as mate, he or she may act as captain of that vessel if the captain is unavailable for command. A mate, 200 tons (NC or OC) may serve as OUPV within the route limitation of the license. A master, 100 or 200 gross tons, may command a vessel within the route and tonnage limitation and also may operate as an OUPV within the route (but not tonnage) limitation. Near-coastal licenses are valid for near-coastal, inland, coastal, and river waters; however, Great Lakes, inland, and river licenses are not accepted for near-coastal waters. Ninety days of service on the Great Lakes qualifies the holder of an inland license up to 200 gross tons for a Great Lakes endorsement.
3. Only U.S. citizens can qualify for licenses for inspected vessels. Noncitizens can qualify only for OUPV licenses.
4. A sail or auxiliary sail endorsement generally requires qualifying time on the respective vessel equal to half the qualifying time needed for the license itself.

CHAPTER 12

Other Requirements for Boats and Crews

RADIOTELEPHONES

Except for certain exemptions, the Vessel Bridge-to-Bridge Radiotelephone Act[1] states that when the following vessels are in navigable waters of the United States, they must have a radiotelephone on board capable of transmitting and receiving on the frequencies within the 156-162 megahertz (MHz) band:

- Power-driven vessels of 20 meters or over in length while navigating;
- Vessels of 100 gross tons or more carrying one or more passengers for hire while navigating;
- Towing vessels of 26 feet or over in length while navigating; and
- Certain dredges and floating plants operating in or near channels or fairways. Vessels identified above that are operating in designated locations in the lower Mississippi River, the Mississippi River–Gulf Outlet and safety fairway, and the Inner Harbor Navigation Canal also must have on board a radiotelephone capable of transmitting and receiving on VHF-FM channel 67 (156.375 MHz).

In addition, when transiting any waters within a Vessel Traffic Service Area (VTS), the vessel must have on board a radiotelephone capable of transmitting and receiving on the frequency designated for that VTS.

SHIP STATION RADIO LICENSES

The Federal Communications Commission requires that each vessel equipped with any of the following types of electronic communications devices have a *ship station license:*[2] VHF-FM radio, radar, EPIRB (emergency position–indicating radio beacon), high-frequency single side band radio, or installed portable radio.

If the EPIRB is a 406 megahertz unit, the FCC requires it to be registered with the National Oceanic and Atmospheric Administration (NOAA), which maintains a twenty-thousand-record database for search-and-rescue identifications. To register a 406 EPIRB, use the card that EPIRB manufacturers pack with each beacon.

If you use a hand-held VHF-FM radio in addition to an installed radio, you do not need a separate license. A hand-held marine radio may be used on a dinghy and in other situations when communications are necessary with the mother ship. In such cases the operator of the hand-held set should include the words "Mobile 1" with the call sign.

However, if the hand-held radio is the only VHF unit for a vessel, you must have a ship station license for it. Furthermore, the regulations forbid keeping a hand-held ashore for communications with your boat or your fleet. In such cases you need a license for a permanent shore-based radio station.

RADIO OPERATOR PERMITS AND LICENSES

In addition to the ship station license requirement, the FCC stipulates that the *operator* may be required to have a *permit* or *license* as outlined below. None of the licenses and permits described authorizes the holder to operate an amateur radio (ham) station. An amateur radio operator license is required to operate a ham station.

Restricted Radiotelephone Operator Permit

In general, an operator of a ship station on a pleasure craft or a boat commanded by an OUPV needs no operator's license or permit to operate in U.S. waters. The ship station license is sufficient. However, if the vessel calls at a foreign port, the station operator must have a license, called a *restricted radiotelephone operator's permit*. This lifetime permit does not require an exam.

Marine Radio Operator Permit

You generally need a marine radio operator permit to operate a ship radio station if:

- The vessel is authorized to carry more than six passengers for hire; or
- The ship is larger than 300 gross tons.

To be eligible for this five-year permit, you must be a legal resident of the United States, be able to receive and transmit spoken messages in English, and pass a twenty-four-question, multiple-choice exam covering basic radio law and operating procedures.

General Radiotelephone Operator's License

This license conveys all of the operating authority of the marine radio operator permit described above. It is required for the following:

- To adjust, maintain, or internally repair FCC-licensed radiotelephone transmitters in the aviation, maritime, and international fixed public radio services;
- To operate any maritime land radio station or compulsorily equipped ship radiotelephone station operating with more than 1,500 watts of peak envelope power; or
- To operate any voluntarily equipped ship and aeronautical (including aircraft) station with more than 1,000 watts of peak envelope power.

To be eligible for this lifetime license, you must be a legal resident of the United States, be able to receive and transmit spoken messages in English, and pass a fifty-question, multiple-choice exam covering basic radio laws, operating procedures, electronics fundamentals, and techniques required to repair and maintain radio transmitters and receivers.

FCC Exams, Licenses, and Forms

A passing score on all exams is 75 percent. For further information, contact any local FCC field office, or the FCC Private Radio Bureau, Licensing Division, Gettysburg, Pennsylvania 17325-7245; 717-337-1212.

The FCC also administers three levels of radiotelegraph operator's certificates and an endorsement for radar repair. For further information, contact the FCC as listed in the paragraph that follows.

For forms, contact the nearest FCC field operations bureau, call 202-632-3676, or write to FCC Forms Distribution Center, 2803 52nd Avenue, Hyattsville, Maryland 20781. You may need any or all of the forms described here:

- To apply for a ship station license, use FCC Form 506. The cost is $35.
- To register a 406 EPIRB, use the FCC registration card that is packed with the beacon.

- To apply for a restricted radiotelephone operator's permit, if you are legally eligible for employment in the United States, use FCC Form 753. The cost is $35.
- If you are not legally eligible for employment in the United States, use FCC Form 755.
- To apply for a marine radio operator permit or a renewal, use FCC Form 756.

For assistance with an application, contact the FCC, Consumer Assistance Branch, 1270 Fairfield Road, Gettysburg, Pennsylvania 17325-7245, or call the FCC at 717-337-1212.

THE FEDERAL DRUG-TESTING PROGRAM

The Coast Guard requires employer participation in a comprehensive drug-testing program mandated by 46 CFR Part 16 and 49 CFR Part 40. Every marine employer, regardless of the firm's size, is required to include each crew member in the program.

A marine employer means the owner, managing operator, charterer, agent, master, or person in charge of a vessel other than a recreational vessel. A crew member (with certain exceptions on fish processing vessels, oceanographic research vessels, and industrial vessels) is described as any person:

- On board a vessel acting under the authority of a license, certificate of registry, or merchant mariner's document, whether or not the individual is a member of the vessel's crew; or
- Engaged or employed on board a vessel owned in the United States that is required by law or regulation to engage, employ, or be operated by an individual holding a license, certificate of registry, or merchant mariner's document.[3]

To ensure that virtually anybody in the industry who operates or helps operate a vessel is covered, the reference adds that "a vessel owned in the United States means any vessel documented or numbered . . . and any vessel owned by a citizen of the United States that is not documented or numbered."

If you are responsible for your company's or your vessel's program, the following is a summary of your requirements.

- Company policy. Keep a readily accessible written policy on drug abuse in the company's files.

- Reports and record keeping. Submit an annual summary of the firm's drug-testing records to the Coast Guard. Keep all drug-testing records on file for five years.
- Employee assistance program. Maintain a written employee assistance program, and conduct one hour of antidrug training for each employee.
- Collection, processing, and review. Utilize approved collection sites and labs, and have results reviewed and interpreted by an approved medical review officer.
- Preemployment testing. Test for anyone hired after December 21, 1990. This includes crew members hired on a full-time, temporary, or seasonal basis, whether for one day or longer.
- Post-accident testing. Require employees to submit specimens after a "serious marine incident," as defined by the Coast Guard.
- "For cause" testing. Arrange tests for employees who you suspect may be using illegal drugs.
- Periodic testing. Tests are required when Coast Guard licenses are renewed.
- Random testing. Randomly test a number of employees throughout each year to equal an annualized rate of 50 percent.

The Penalties for Noncompliance

Violators of the regulation are subject to permanent revocation or a two-year suspension of licenses, certificates of registry, and merchant mariner's documents.

You can obtain a list of approved sites, labs, and medical review officers from the nearest Coast Guard Regional Exam Center and set up your own program. However, many small charter operators enroll with organizations that administer every requirement except for providing the specimens. The National Association of Charterboat Operators (NACO) sponsors The Maritime Consortium, Inc., which accepts NACO and non-NACO members (P.O. Box 25345, Alexandria, VA 22313-5345; phone 800-775-6985).

PERSONAL FLOTATION DEVICES (PFDs)[4]

Beginning in May 1995, boats of *any* size must be equipped with one Type I, II, III, or V PFD for each person aboard. PFD categories are:

- Type I—Offshore life jacket. This PFD must have a minimum of 22 pounds buoyancy (11 pounds for a child). It will turn most wearers faceup.

- Type II—Near-shore life jacket. This PFD must have a minimum of 15.5 pounds buoyancy (11 pounds for a child). It will turn some wearers faceup.
- Type III—Flotation aid. This PFD must have the same buoyancy as the Type II. Most wearers can place themselves in a faceup position when wearing it.
- Type V—Special use device. This PFD must have performance equal to a Type I, II, or III. To be acceptable, it has to be worn when under way.

HAND-PORTABLE FIRE EXTINGUISHERS[5]

Each hand-portable fire extinguisher is classified by letters and a roman numeral. The letters designate the type of fire or fires it is expected to extinguish. For example, Class A extinguishers should be used only on Class A fires. Class AB extinguishers may be used on fires involving both Class A and B fires, or a combination of both. The roman numeral indicates the relative size or efficiency of the extinguisher. The numeral I indicates the smallest size and V the largest. Fire classifications are:

- Class A. Fires involving common combustible solids, such as wood and paper.
- Class B. Gasoline, oil, and grease fires.
- Class C. Electrical fires.
- Class D. Fires involving combustible metals, such as potassium, sodium, magnesium, and zinc.

Coast Guard–approved, hand-portable fire extinguishers must be carried on any motor-powered vessel that has one or more of the following features:

- An inboard engine;
- A closed compartment under a thwart or seats where portable fuel tanks are stored;
- Double bottoms not sealed to the hull or which are not completely filled with flotation materials;
- Closed living spaces;
- Closed stowage compartments in which combustible or flammable materials are stored; and/or
- Permanently installed fuel tanks.

For vessels 65 feet or under in length that require hand-portable fire extinguishers, the requirements are as follows:

- Vessels under 26 feet in length must have one Type B-1 extinguisher. However, if an approved fixed fire-extinguishing system is installed in machinery spaces, no Type B-1 is required.
- Vessels at least 26 feet and less than 40 feet in length must have at least two Type B-1 or at least one Type B-2 extinguishers. If an approved fixed fire-extinguishing system is installed, only one Type B-1 extinguisher is required.
- Vessels at least 40 feet and not more than 65 feet in length must have at least three Type B-1, or at least one Type B-1, *plus* one Type B-2 extinguisher. If an approved fixed fire-extinguishing system is installed, only two Type B-1 extinguishers are required.

For vessels more than 65 feet in length, the following is the minimum number of hand-portable extinguishers:[6]

- Not over 50 gross tons—at least one Type B-2 extinguisher.
- Over 50 gross tons but not over 100 gross tons—at least two Type B-2 extinguishers.
- Over 100 gross tons but not over 500 gross tons—at least three Type B-2 extinguishers.
- Over 500 gross tons but not over 1,000 gross tons—at least six Type B-2 extinguishers.
- Over 1,000 gross tons—at least eight Type B-2 extinguishers.

VISUAL DISTRESS SIGNALS[7]

In addition to the requirements for inspected vessels, all recreational vessels 16 feet or more in length (with exceptions listed below), and vessels carrying six or fewer passengers for hire or charter passengers, must be equipped with visual distress signals for day and night use. Vessels less than 16 feet in length must have signals for night use (between sunset and sunrise).

Applicable waters are offshore, near shore, the Great Lakes, territorial seas, and those waters connected directly to the Great Lakes and the territorial seas, up to a point where a body of water is less than 2 miles wide. An example of the latter would be a river mouth that is less than 2 miles wide.

Exceptions are (1) boats participating in organized parades, regattas, or races; (2) manually propelled vessels; and (3) sailboats of completely open construction, not equipped with propulsion machinery, and under 26 feet in length.

Any combination of the signals listed below, when carried in the required number, may be used to meet both day and night requirements. Three day signals and one night signal are required. For example, two hand-held red flares and one parachute red flare meet both day and night requirements. Three hand-held orange smoke signals with one electric distress light also meet both day and night requirements. For day use only the requirements are as follows:

- Three floating orange smoke distress signals;
- Three hand-held orange smoke distress signals; or
- One orange flag.

For night use only the requirement is:

- Electric distress lantern for boats.

For both day and night use:

- Three pistol-projected parachute red flares;
- Three hand-held rocket-propelled parachute red flares;
- Three red aerial pyrotechnic flares; or
- Three hand-held red flares.

EMERGENCY POSITION-INDICATING RADIO BEACONS (EPIRBs)[8]

The Class A EPIRB (121.5 MHz) was developed to transmit emergency signals from distressed vessels to satellites and overflying aircraft. Although these beacons have saved many lives, they have limitations. For example, they are effective only when a satellite can communicate with the transmitting beacon and a ground station at the same time. In addition, there have often been no overflying aircraft to receive the signals of activated EPIRBs. Perhaps most importantly, when first activated, their early transmissions often are not identified as emergency signals because of the amount of noise on 121.5 MHz.

The Type I (406 MHz) EPIRB, on the other hand, was specifically designed for global satellite coverage. It provides a clearer signal and a more accurate position than the Class A, and each beacon has a unique identifying code which links it to the owner and the owner's vessel once it is registered. Not surprisingly, the Coast Guard would like a Type I EPIRB on every offshore vessel, and so would every skipper. However, the cost, at about $1,000, is prohibitive for many boat owners.

At the present time, a Class A EPIRB manufactured on or after October 1, 1988, is required for inspected small passenger vessels operating on ocean and coastwise service more than 20 nautical miles from a harbor of safe refuge. The Coast Guard has proposed that this requirement be upgraded to a Type I EPIRB. EPIRBs are not currently required for uninspected vessels.

For larger vessels, the International Maritime Organization requires Type I EPIRBs on vessels subject to the SOLAS Convention. Certain commercial fishing vessels also must be equipped with the Type I beacons.

OTHER SAFETY EQUIPMENT

Although a captain is required by law to keep certain safety equipment aboard, you should remember that the requirements are a bare minimum. For example, if you were the skipper of a 30-foot boat, what would you do if you used your only two extinguishers to suppress a fire, and the fire reignited? Or what would you do if your vessel was dead in the water, and you fired your minimum supply of flares and smoke without being seen? Or consider the following case, where the Coast Guard decided a captain needed more than the minimum:

A dive-boat operator got caught in a storm with three divers down and four other members of the dive group on board. He took the passengers to shore (nearly 2 miles away), notified the Coast Guard, borrowed a bigger vessel, and returned for the divers. By the time he arrived, a Coast Guard vessel had safely picked up the divers.

At the subsequent hearing, the dive-boat skipper pled no contest to several charges, including a charge of negligently failing to monitor the local weather conditions by all available means. Here is a summarized version of the investigating officer's comments made during a telephone interview:

> It's really important to get this across to everybody concerned. After (the dive-boat skipper) departed the dock, the National Weather Service spotted a very severe storm on radar, moving rapidly toward (the skipper's location). NOAA Weather Radio and other stations reported the information with a detailed follow-up an hour later. Meanwhile (the skipper) was out in his boat on a clear day, incapable of knowing what those agencies were transmitting. If he had even had a $20 Radio Shack receiver, he could have heard the broadcast. With that information a reasonable person would not have started (the) dive.[9]

As a result of all charges, the skipper received an outright suspension of his license for eighteen months. He reported that he now keeps a VHF radiotelephone on each of his dive-boats, even though nothing in writing lists such equipment as mandatory.

INLAND NAVIGATION RULES

The operator of each self-propelled vessel that is 12 meters (39.4 feet) or more in length is required to carry on board, and maintain for ready reference, a copy of the Inland Navigation Rules ("Rules of the Road").

PASSPORTS

If your boat will depart U.S. waters, a passport and visa might be required, depending upon the country. For passport information, try the number for county, state, or federal information in the government offices section of the telephone book. Post offices have passport renewals forms and any travel agent should also know where to apply for a passport.

PROFESSIONAL QUALIFICATIONS OF CAPTAIN AND CREW

The Armed Forces hold a commanding officer responsible for everything his unit does or fails to do. Period.

The same philosophy applies to a captain afloat. The captain is responsible to make every decision and carry out, or have carried out, every action. The captain is a god, but godliness ends upon returning to port, because every decision and action of command is subject to review and adjudication.

If you are looking for a captain to hire, first seek strong credentials—a captain's license from the Coast Guard; a substantiated, verifiable résumé; and credible references. Then be sure you are entirely comfortable with your prospective captain's personality. Finally, come to grips with how much autonomy and use of your funds a captain will need in order to take out passengers on your boat, and how much you are willing to give. At that stage you are ready to strike a financial deal, seal it with a contract, and protect your investment with insurance.

Be sure the contract provides an escape clause in case your captain proves to be less than satisfactory on the water. During interviews for this chapter, I remarked to Mike Bomar of Capt. Mike's Watersports that I assumed he had no problems finding good captains to help him run his parasail vessels, and he broke out in laughter. Then he said, "It's difficult to find a good captain. Regardless of what they say and what is on their résumé, you don't know what they are like until they have been out on the water with your customers."

I asked a charter fleet operator what he expected of his captains. He said, "Seamanship and navigational ability are important, but our captains learn the routes quickly, and navigate them almost automatically. What they can never do is to expect passengers to be automatically comfortable and happy." He explained that it takes no more than an off-guard comment, an accidental expression, or a perceived lack of concern to lose a customer's goodwill permanently. "No goodwill means no return business and no referrals," he said. "That ultimately means no business."

Here is a positive example: One steamy summer morning at Fort Myers, Florida, I watched a couple serving as captain and mate on a Hatteras 48. They rose at 0500, washed and dried the weather decks, and changed to fresh white uniforms. They cooked breakfast and served the passengers (grandfather and grandmother, father and mother, and two children) from 0600 to 0630. Leaving fresh coffee on the dining table and the television on, the skipper took the helm and his mate went to handle the lines.

Smaller yachts were docked alongside the seawall forward and aft, and the wind was adverse, as the two began working the Hatteras out with springs. The captain had to go on deck to check conditions several times. Things turned iffy and they had to start over. But in due time they cleared the dock and the harbor. No screaming, no yelling, not even loud talking, and no running. The passengers, unaware of the difficulty, were still sitting in their chairs in the dining room, with delicate coffee cups perched on the table. My last view was of the mate washing and drying her hands from a freshwater spigot on deck before she went inside to offer fresh coffee.

QUALIFICATIONS TO PERFORM MARRIAGES

How valid is a marriage performed by a captain at sea? The captain's authority to perform marriages is well established in the common law of admiralty. However, that validity may depend upon documentation from the ship's log. For a permanent record of the marriage, a true copy or a certified copy of the log entry should be recorded in a county clerk's office after making landfall (or in an appropriate functionary's office if abroad).

A civil or religious marriage might avoid possible legal difficulties in proving validity of marriages at sea. A clergyman who is a skipper can perform marriages in state waters. So can a notary public, if marriages by notaries are legal in the state where performed. Generally, all it takes is a marriage license (procured by the prospective bride and groom), which the clergyman or notary fills out after performing the ceremony. By all means make an appropriate log entry. You can obtain a notary-public commission directly from the state.

SUMMARY

1. Certain vessels are required in writing to be equipped with one or more radiotelephones, but a prudent charter operator will install a radio on almost any boat that carries passengers for hire or charter passengers.

2. You must have a ship station license for radios and EPIRBs, but the operator must have a license only when transmitting in foreign waters.
3. Every charter operator who is an employer or skipper must participate in the federal drug-testing program.
4. A captain is a god at sea, but every decision is subject to review upon returning to port. The captain is responsible for everything that he or she does or fails to do.
5. A captain's first responsibility is for the safety of the vessel, passengers, and crew.
6. A successful charter-boat captain places the happiness of the passengers immediately after safety considerations.

CHAPTER 13

Coast Guard Investigations and Hearings

The Coast Guard can make an administrative determination to issue a license, document, or certificate to a person, and it can also make an administrative decision to suspend or revoke those instruments. The Coast Guard takes these actions by conducting investigations and hearings for revocation and suspension of the instrument concerned.[1] These are actions against the *instrument*, not the individual.

Such actions are separate from those which an officer in charge, marine inspection (OCMI), may take against certificates of documentation and certificates of inspection issued for vessels. This chapter concerns only the licenses, documents, and certificates issued to persons. The term *license* used in the chapter refers to any of the three instruments.

The Coast Guard explains that suspension and revocation methods were not created as a form of punishment, but as a way of helping to maintain a minimum level of professional competence after issuance of the documents. Such follow-up procedure is a continuing program, which the agency carries out by investigating and holding hearing procedures in cases where minimum competence appears questionable. Because the purpose is remedial rather than punitive, the procedures are different from those in civil or criminal court.

An investigation doesn't mean that the operator's boat automatically will be seized and held for an *in rem* proceeding (action against "the thing," meaning the vessel). If the issue is simply over the captain's right to hold the license, the result could be an administrative law hearing. However, the Coast Guard may also initiate a civil penalty against any operator—licensed or unlicensed—and can proceed *in rem* to ensure the penalty will be paid.

An investigation may be precipitated by any of the following:

- If a casualty occurs due to an accident or collision;
- If another charter operator reports an apparent violation of the regulations;
- If a passenger, crew member, or other witness reports an apparent violation of regulations;
- If the Coast Guard or other agency gains evidence during a boarding that appears to warrant action against the license; or
- If by any other means the Coast Guard has reasonable grounds to suspect a violation.

THE INVESTIGATING OFFICER'S ROLE

The first job of the investigating officer (IO) is to find out what happened, in order to prevent it from happening again. So when a marine casualty occurs, the IO might appear to be sincerely trying to help. But any license holder involved must remember that the IO is bound to pursue any case against the license that appears to be warranted.

This poses a dilemma. All hands involved in an incident are required by law to help the IO determine the cause.[2] Yet, if possible wrongdoing surfaces, that same IO begins a second investigation, against the license. Part 5 of 46 CFR states that no admission a person makes during an investigation may be used against that person during a subsequent administrative hearing, except to prove impeachment. But the IO still *knows* the evidence has been uncovered. If the licensee appears to be guilty of something, the IO wants to prove it, and has full authority to proceed.

Does the IO's dual mission turn investigations into witch-hunts? Not necessarily, because the Coast Guard assigns senior, experienced officers as OCMIs and expects them to require their IOs to take balanced approaches. After all, the Coast Guard is neither empowered nor motivated to attempt to force every charter operator out of business.

What does a license holder do when an IO starts asking questions? If there's any chance of facing charges against the license, or more, the license holder had better tread carefully. Although the Coast Guard at that stage is not required to read any rights against self-incrimination, a skipper should be quick to insist upon talking to an attorney before making any statement.

During the investigation, the IO has the power of subpoena, as well as the power to:[3]

- Prefer charges. This sets the stage for a revocation and suspension hearing before an administrative law judge.

- Accept voluntary surrender of the license. In this case, the skipper permanently relinquishes all rights to the license in exchange for not having to appear at a hearing.
- Accept voluntary deposit of the license. In case of possible mental or physical incompetence, the license may be deposited, with a written agreement specifying the conditions under which it will be returned. If the incompetence derives from drugs, the license can only be voluntarily surrendered. A surrender is permanent, while a deposit can be temporary.
- Refer the case to others for further action. It can go to the commandant, or to any OCMI located near the person under investigation or the witnesses.
- Give a written warning. This becomes a permanent record, but so does a record of hearing. Sometimes a license holder will accept a written warning as an alternative in order to continue in business. In case of refusal, the IO normally will prefer charges.
- Close the case.

Possible Charges

The possible charges that the investigating officer can prefer are as follows:[4]

- Misconduct, negligence, or incompetence, when acting under authority of the license. Misconduct is violation of a rule or regulation. An OUPV who takes seven passengers for hire is violating a regulation in the Code of Federal Regulations and is guilty of misconduct. Negligence stems from an act that a reasonable and prudent person of the same station, under the same circumstances, would not commit. It can also be a failure to perform in a situation where the other person would. Charges of negligence can be subjective, based upon what the Coast Guard believes another captain would or would not have done. Incompetence is the inability to perform required duties. It can be due to professional deficiencies, physical disability, mental incapacity, or any combination of these. A skipper who cannot operate an onboard radar may be guilty of incompetence; so may a captain who is under the influence of alcohol.
- Violation of laws or regulations that apply when acting under authority of the license. A charge here can be much more serious than a misconduct charge, because it leaves the skipper wide open to criminal charges by a U.S. attorney. The law referred to is Title 46 of the U.S. Code, Subtitle II, which covers shipping, as well as "any other law or regulation intended to promote marine safety or protect navigable waters."

"Acting under authority of the license" refers to being employed in the service of a vessel when either the law or employer requires a license. It applies on board and ashore. Don't let this term sneak up and bite you. Let's say the Coast Guard doesn't require a license for a charter operation, but the employer does. So far as the Coast Guard is concerned, it's the same as if *they* required it, so all rules and regulations apply. A captain is also acting under authority of the license any time he or she is engaged is official matters concerning the license. This includes such actions as taking exams for endorsements or renewals, and applying for replacement licenses.

- Conviction for a dangerous drug law violation, use of a dangerous drug, or addiction to the use of dangerous drugs. (This charge is not contingent upon the operator's acting under authority of the license.)

Specifications

To prefer any charge, the IO must prepare one or more specifications. A specification is the act the investigating officer believes you committed that, if proven, will find you guilty of the charge.

THE ROLE OF THE ADMINISTRATIVE LAW JUDGE

The judge is hired to conduct hearings as an administrative law judge,[5] not to try civil or criminal cases. Administrative law judges are civilians, qualified to work for the Coast Guard under 5 U.S.C. 556(b). These individuals work for the commandant, under staff supervision of the chief administrative law judge in Washington.

The administrative law judge is not something the Coast Guard invented. There are some eight hundred of these judges who are competitive career civil servants. The Coast Guard employs about ten of them.

The Office of Personnel Management selects an administrative law judge from a register created by examinations. (Yes, even administrative law judges must sit for exams in order to get their Coast Guard tickets.) To be eligible for the exam, a candidate must have seven years of practice—in law, administrative law, or the equivalent. If successful with the written exam, the candidate must pass a personal interview with other administrative law judges. Then he or she is eligible to sit on a Coast Guard bench.

The judge's job under the law is to help the commandant maintain minimum professional competence of license holders. To accomplish this task, the judge has the authority to admonish; suspend with or without probation; or revoke a license, document, or certificate.

THE STAGES OF A HEARING

If both sides agree, the judge may hold a prehearing conference to settle or simplify the issues.[6] By this stage, the license holder ought to have a good idea of whether the IO wants revocation, suspension, or admonishment, or whether the IO simply thinks the judge ought to hear the case. The operator also might gain insight into how the judge views the case. By the time a prehearing conference takes place, both sides have a reasonable idea of what might and might not be proved. Plea bargaining might be in order. At a prehearing conference, the license holder must remember that any admission or statement he or she makes will not be admissible in evidence at a hearing for any reason.

At the administrative hearing, as the representative of the Coast Guard, the IO has the burden of proof. The judge, although not required to adhere strictly to the rules of evidence, uses the Federal Rules of Evidence as a guide. If the license holder has no professional counsel, the judge allows more latitude in presenting the case than that offered to counsel. And remember: If the license holder doesn't show up, the hearing takes place anyway.

The license holder can plead guilty, not guilty, or no contest. A guilty plea means, "I did it." A not guilty plea means, "I'm not saying whether or not I did it. If you think I did, prove it." A no-contest plea means, "I'm not saying whether or not I did it, but I'll let you say I did it."

No-contest pleas are often used in plea bargaining, wherein the license holder tells the investigating officer (after consultation with the attorney), "You guys might spend a lot of time and money and never prove this. I'll plead no contest in exchange for. . . ." This might give the IO an opportunity to reply, "Very well, plead guilty to this one and. . . ." And so it goes.

If a charge is "not proved," the judge will enter an order dismissing it. If it is found "proved," the judge will enter an order specifying whether the license is:

1. Revoked;
2. Suspended outright for a specified period after surrender;
3. Suspended for a specified period, but placed on probation for a specified period; or
4. Suspended outright for a specified period, followed by a specified period of suspension on probation.

(For guidelines on orders used by administrative law judges, see appendix H.)

If the judge finds a charge of *misconduct* has been proved because of wrongful possession, use, sale, or association with dangerous drugs, he or she *must* order the license revoked.[7] The only exception concerns marijuana: the license holder must convince the judge that (1) he or she had been merely experimenting, and (2) he or she is "cured," and will not repeat the offense.

If the judge finds that a license holder has been convicted for violation of a dangerous drug law, use of a dangerous drug, or addiction to the use of dangerous drugs, he or she *must* revoke the license. Note the difference here. If the charge is *misconduct*, and the substance is marijuana, the judge has a choice. If the charge is *conviction*, there is no choice.

The IO will urge revocation for anyone he or she believes has committed one of the following acts or offenses:[8]

1. Assault with a dangerous weapon;
2. Misconduct resulting in loss of life or serious injury;
3. Rape or sexual molestation;
4. Murder or attempted murder;
5. Mutiny;
6. Perversion;
7. Sabotage;
8. Smuggling of aliens;
9. Incompetence;
10. Interference with the master, ship's officers, or government officials in their performance of official duties;
11. Wrongful destruction of ship's property;
12. An act or prior record indicating that continuation of the license would be a threat to the safety of life or property, or detrimental to good discipline.

Post Hearing

If a license holder receives an adverse finding, five possible avenues remain:

1. Modification of the judge's order. If the proceeding is based upon a conviction for a dangerous drug law violation, and the respondent submits a specific court order to the effect that the conviction has been unconditionally set aside, the respondent can request that the judge rescind the order.
2. Petition to reopen hearing. The respondent can petition on the basis of newly discovered evidence, *or* on the basis that the respondent had been unable to appear at the hearing through no personal fault and due to circumstances beyond his or her control.

3. Appeal to the commandant. Within thirty days of the judge's written decision, the respondent can appeal to the Coast Guard commandant, who will consider only the following matters: rulings on motions or objections which were not waived during the proceedings, clear errors in the record, or jurisdictional questions.

   If the offense was not one of those requiring mandatory revocation, or one of the other causes for revocation, the respondent might get a temporary license, pending results of the appeal.
4. Appeal to the National Transportation Safety Board (NTSB). In cases of suspension or revocation, if the commandant's decision on appeal remains adverse, the respondent can appeal to the NTSB within ten days. If the offense was not one of those that would prohibit issuing a temporary license, the commandant may issue a stay. This could allow another temporary license until the NTSB completes its review.
5. Go to the circuit court of appeals. A respondent with a strong case who has time (and money for legal fees) may consider going to the federal court system.[9]

As early as a year later, a person whose license was revoked or surrendered because of minor offenses may apply for a new license. If the license was lost because of a major offense, the minimum time might be three years. However, each individual has the option to try any time after one year. The commandant's ultimate decision depends upon:

- Letters and recommendations from employers.
- Any other information that might be cause for approval of a new license.
- The recommendation of the OCMI through whom the respondent forwards the application. (The OCMI is normally the IO's immediate superior.)

Of course, losing a license is serious business if you are a charter operator who depends upon it for your income, but it doesn't always mean the business has to shut down. If you have a small family-run operation, you might see to it that your spouse gets qualifying time and a license. The same goes for children who are eighteen or older. Another option is to turn the business into a bareboat operation.

Consider the case in which loss of a license opened up a new horizon for a dive-boat operator interviewed for this book. He had been taking divers out on his boat while his wife ran the dive shop ashore. When his license was suspended, he bought two more boats, hired three captains, and moved ashore to run a greatly expanded dive-certification and open-water program. He even joined his students on their dives, letting his hired captain stay aboard the boat as the captain is required to do. This is the kind of financial leverage discussed earlier that every charter operator can live with.

SUMMARY

1. The Coast Guard maintains minimum proficiency of its licensed charter captains by administrative law investigations and hearings, with the overall goal being to promote marine safety.
2. Under the administrative law process, possible charges against a license, document, or certificate are misconduct, negligence, incompetence, violation of laws and regulations, and conviction for violating dangerous drug laws.
3. An investigation and administrative law hearing can result in voluntary surrender of a license, voluntary deposit of a license, dismissal of charges, admonition, suspension, or revocation.
4. Appeals from adverse findings of an administrative law judge follow a designated chain, up to and including the federal court system.

APPENDIX A

Selecting A Marine Surveyor

Obviously a qualified, objective marine surveyor is important to buyer, seller, and carrier. Some carriers employ a staff of in-house marine surveyors. In most cases, however, you will choose your own surveyor.

The person you choose should possess more qualifications than just a business card, a local license to do business, or a captain's license issued by the Coast Guard. To begin with, the American Boat and Yacht Council publishes forty-five standards totaling four hundred and fifty pages that cover everything from a boat's deck hardware to its fuel and electrical systems. A competent marine surveyor should have a comfortable working knowledge of them all.

Additionally, a surveyor should know national Fire Protection Association standards, the Coast Guard's safety requirements, and be familiar with construction standards, such as those of the American Bureau of Shipping and Lloyd's.[1]

Although many competent surveyors choose not to join a professional organization, others do. An overview of two such organizations—both of which have programs to certify or accredit their members, and stress professional ethics—follows:[2]

The National Association of Marine Surveyors (NAMS). NAMS was founded in 1961. Each applicant must be sponsored by a current member and must have at least five years of experience as a full-time surveyor in the professional practice of hull, machinery, marine facility, cargo, yacht, or small craft surveying. The applicant must pass a written exam and be approved by a regional screening committee. A successful applicant is awarded the title of Certified Marine Surveyor (CMS). NAMS has an associate and apprentice membership program and lists over four hundred members of all categories.

The Society of Accredited Marine Surveyors (SAMS). SAMS was founded in 1987. Applicants must have a minimum of five years experience and must pass an oral and written examination given by the testing committee. A successful applicant is awarded the title of Accredited Marine Surveyor (AMS). He or she may carry designations for yachts and small craft, engines only (not solely gasoline engines), blue water, tug and barge, fishing vessel, and cargo. SAMS has a surveyor associate and affiliate member program and lists over four hundred members of all categories.

Many marine insurance companies keep a list of surveyors whose work they know and their underwriters will accept. For example, BOAT/U.S. Marine Insurance maintains a referral listing of surveyors which can be obtained by calling 800-283-2883.

APPENDIX B

Boarding Checklist (Six-pack)

This list was summarized from a compilation of charter vessel regulations provided by the Coast Guard Marine Safety Office (MSO) in Norfolk, Virginia, and printed in the National Association of Passenger Vessel Operators' newsletter, "The NACO Report." It should be updated periodically with your nearest MSO and should be used prior to getting under way.

CAPTAIN AND CREW REQUIREMENTS

- Is operator a licensed OUPV or master, with license in possession?
- Is operator licensed for water to be navigated (inland, Great Lakes, near- coastal, oceans)?
- If voyage is to be over twelve hours, are enough operators aboard to stand two watches?
- Are captain and crew enrolled in a drug-testing program which includes random testing at 50 percent annually?
- Is there evidence of a program for preemployment, serious marine incident, reasonable cause, and periodic drug tests?
- Does the company maintain one-year (negative results) and five-year (positive results) drug-testing records?

LIFESAVING EQUIPMENT

- Is a Type I approved life preserver of suitable size for each person (or approved hybrid PFD) aboard and readily accessible?
- Is retroreflective material on each life preserver?
- Is lifesaving equipment marked showing Coast Guard approval numbers?
- Is throwable lifesaving equipment immediately accessible?
- Is a throwable life ring aboard and accessible?
- Is all lifesaving equipment in serviceable condition?
- Are personal flotation device lights (for oceans, coastwise, near-coastal, and Great Lakes service) in place?

SAFETY

- Is an emergency checklist posted?
- Has a safety orientation been given to the passengers?
- Is the required minimum number of serviceable, portable fire extinguishers (for vessels up to 65 feet) aboard?
- Are fire extinguishers Coast Guard approved or listed by Underwriters' Laboratories (UL) for marine use?
- Do all fire extinguishers have nameplates attached?
- If equipped with radar, is it operated competently when under way?

NAVIGATION AND PILOTHOUSE

- Is a copy of the Inland Navigation Rules aboard?
- If vessel is 26 feet in length or over, does it have a bridge-to-bridge radio for use on Channel 13 (156.65 MHz)?
- Is there a valid radio station license?
- Are required navigation lights and an anchor light installed and working?
- Does equipment include the required sound-producing devices?

OIL POLLUTION PREVENTION

- If vessel is longer than 26 feet, is a 5-inch by 8-inch Prohibited Discharge Warning placard posted in the machinery space or at the bilge pump control station?
- Are oily mixtures retained on board for subsequent discharge at a reception facility?

GARBAGE POLLUTION PREVENTION

- If vessel is longer than 26 feet, are 4-inch by 9-inch durable Marpol placards, with ⅛-inch letters, prominently displayed in sufficient numbers?
- If vessel is longer than 40 feet, does it contain a written waste management plan?
- Do captain, crew, and passengers comply with required disposal of plastics, paper, rags, glass, metal, and other items?

SEWAGE CONTROL

(If Vessel Has Toilet Facilities Installed)

- Is each one a certified marine sanitation device (MSD), Type I, II, or III?
- Does sewage discharge to a holding or treatment tank?
- For Type I or II devices, is an identification placard attached?
- If it is a Type I device, was it installed before January 30, 1980?
- If it is a Type III device, are there adequate pumpout arrangements?
- Is the MSD overboard shutoff valve kept closed when within 3 miles of shore?

APPENDIX C

Examination Subjects for Selected U.S. Coast Guard Licenses

This table was extracted from Table 10.910-2, Subjects For Deck Licenses, in 46 CFR 10.910. It lists examination subjects for licenses as operator of uninspected passenger vessels (OUPV, or "six-pack" operator), and master of inspected vessals to 200 gross tons, as shown in the column designations that follow:

Column 1. Master, oceans/near coastal, and mate, near coastal, 200 gross tons (includes master, near coastal, 100 gross tons).

Column 2. Operator, uninspected passenger vessels, near coastal.

Column 3. Operator, uninspected passenger vessels, Great Lakes/inland.

Column 4. Master or mate, Great Lakes/inland, 200 gross tons (includes master, Great Lakes/inland, 100 gross tons).

An "X" in table denotes exam subject. A number refers to notes at end of table.

EXAMINATION TOPICS	1	2	3	4
NAVIGATION AND POSITION DETERMINATION:				
Piloting:				
Distance Off	x	x	x	x
Bearing Problems	x	x	x	x
Fix or Running Fix	x	x	x	x
Chart Navigation	x	x	x	x
Dead Reckoning	x	x	x	x
Celestial Observations:				
Latitude by Meridian Transit (Sun Only)	1			
Fix or Running Fix (Sun Only)	1			
Times of Celestial Phenomena:				
Time of Meridian Transit (Sun Only)	1			
Second Estimate Meridian Transit				
Zone Time Sun Rise/Set/Twilight	1			
Electronic Navigation	x	x	x	x
Instruments and Accessories	x	x	x	x
Aids to Navigation	x	x	x	x
Charts, Navigation Publications, and Notices to Mariners	x	x	x	x

SEAMANSHIP:				
Marlinspike Seamanship	x	x	x	x
Purchases, Blocks and Tackle	x			x
WATCHKEEPING:				
COLREGS	x	x	2	2
Inland Navigational Rules	x	x	x	x
Basic Principles, Watchkeeping	x			x
RADAR EQUIPMENT:				
Radar Observer Certificate	1			
COMPASS—MAGNETIC AND GYRO:				
Principles of Magnetic Compass				x
Gyro Compass Error/Correction	3			3
Magnetic Compass Error/Correction	x	x	x	x
Determination of Compass Error				
Azimuth (Sun Only)	1			
Amplitude (Sun Only)	1			
Terrestrial Observation	x	x	x	x
METEOROLOGY AND OCEANOGRAPHY:				
Characteristics of Weather Systems	x	x	x	x
Weather Charts and Reports	x			
Tides and Tidal Currents				
Terms and Definitions	x	x	x	x
Publications	x	x	x	x
Calculations	x	x	x	x
SHIP MANEUVERING AND HANDLING:				
Shiphandling in Rivers, Estuaries	x	x	x	x
Maneuvering in Shallow Water	x	x	x	x
Interaction with Bank/Passing Ship	x	x	x	x
Berthing and Unberthing	x	x	x	x
Anchoring and Mooring	x	x	x	x
Dragging, Clearing Fouled Anchors	x			x
Heavy Weather Operations	x	x	x	x
Maneuvering for Launching of Lifeboats and Liferafts in Heavy Weather	x			
Receiving Survivors from Lifeboats and Liferafts	x			
General: Turn Circle, Pivot Point, Advance, Transfer	x	x	x	x

Wake Reduction	x	x	x	x
Towing Operations	x			x
SHIP STABILITY, CONTROL, AND DAMAGE CONTROL:				
Principles of Ship Construction	x			x
Trim and Stability	x			x
Damage, Trim, and Stability	3			
Stability, Trim, and Stress Calculation	3			
Vessel Structural Members	3			3
Damage Control		3		
SHIP POWER PLANTS:				
Marine Power Plant Operating Principles	3			3
Marine Engineering Terms	3			3
Small Engine Operations and Maintenance	x	x	x	x
CARGO HANDLING AND STOWAGE:				
Cargo Stowage and Security, Including Cargo Gear	3			3
Ballasting, Tank Cleaning, and Gas-free Operations				x
Load on Top Procedures				x
FIRE PREVENTION AND FIRE-FIGHTING APPLIANCES:				
Organization and Fire Drills	x			x
Classes and Chemistry of Fire	x	x	x	x
Fire-fighting Systems	x			x
Fire-fighting Equipment and Regulations	3			3
Fire-fighting Equipment and Regulations for T-Boats	x			x
Basic Fire-fighting and Prevention	x	x	x	x
EMERGENCY PROCEDURES:				
Collision	x	x		x
Temporary Repairs	x	x	x	x
Passenger/Crew Safety in Emergency	x	x	x	x
Fire or Explosion	x	x	x	x
Abandon Ship Procedures	x	x	x	x
Rescuing Survivors from Ships/Aircraft in Distress	x			x
Man Overboard Procedures	x	x	x	x
Emergency Towing	x			
MEDICAL CARE:				
First Aid	x	x	x	x

MARITIME LAW:				
International Maritime Law				
SOLAS	3			
National Maritime Law				
Load Lines	x			3
Certification and Documentation of Vessels	x	x	x	x
Rules and Regulations for Inspected Vessels	3			3
Rules and Regulations for Inspected T-Boats	x			x
Rules and Regulations for Uninspected Vessels	x	x	x	x
Pollution Prevention Regulations	x	x	x	x
Licensing and Certification of Seamen	x	x	x	x
Shipment and Discharge, Manning	x			
SHIPBOARD MANAGEMENT AND TRAINING:				
Ship Sanitation	x	x	x	x
Vessel Alteration/Repair—Hot Work	x			
Safety	x	x	x	x
SHIP'S BUSINESS:				
Certificates and Documents Required	x	x	x	x
COMMUNICATIONS:				
Radiotelephone Communications	x	x	x	x
Signals: Storm/Wreck/Special	x	x	x	x
LIFESAVING:				
Survival at Sea	x			
Lifesaving Appliance Regulations	3			3
Lifesaving Appliance Regulations for T-Boats	x			x
Lifesaving Appliance Operation	3	x	x	3
Lifesaving Appliance Operations for T-Boats	x			x
SAIL/AUXILIARY SAIL VESSELS ADDENDUM (Note 4) Any other subject considered necessary to establish the applicant's proficiency.	x	x	x	x

Notes:

1. For ocean routes only.
2. Take COLREGS if license not limited to non-COLREG waters.
3. For licenses over 100 gross tons.
4. Sail vessel safety precautions, rules of the road, operations, heavy weather procedures, navigation, maneuvering, and sailing terminology. Applicants for sail/auxiliary sail endorsements to master, mate, or operator of uninspected passenger vessels licenses are also tested in the subjects contained in this addendum.

APPENDIX D

Inspection and Certification Checklist

This is a sample list. Requirements could vary. Refer to 46 CFR Part T, located in 46 CFR 166-199, for specifics.

1. Submit application (CG-3752).
2. Dry-dock vessel for USCG examination at a mutually agreed time and place.
3. Submit plans, blueprints, or sketches of vessel and systems. Include listing and description of all basic machinery and electrical equipment.
4. Provide two means of access or emergency escape to all compartments over 12 feet in length.
5. Provide adequate ventilation to all closed spaces.
6. Provide fume-tight separation of machinery and fuel tank spaces from accommodation spaces.
7. For vessels that fish exclusively, provide rails with maximum 12-inch spacing of courses at periphery of all decks accessible to passengers. For excursion vessels, fill in the rails completely.
8. Provide guards over all exposed moving machinery.
9. Provide freeing ports for well decks and/or scuppers for cockpits.
10. Provide a collision bulkhead.
11. Provide watertight bulkheads with one compartment subdivision if over forty-nine passengers are to be carried.
12. Provide stability data.
13. Provide watertight hatches or 12-inch trunks and 6-inch or 3-inch door coamings at weather-deck openings in deckhouse.
14. Provide sea valves at all hull penetrations within 6 inches of waterline and below and reach rods where needed for accessibility.
15. Provide USCG-approved life floats or buoyant apparatus for route and service intended.
16. Remove unapproved or unmaintained lifesaving gear from the vessel.
17. Provide water lights and manila painter (hemp rope), 24 feet by 2 inches, or its equivalent for buoyant apparatus. Also provide two paddles for life floats if carried.
18. Provide one approved-type life preserver for each person on board and an additional 10 percent of the total in child's life preservers.
19. Provide topside stowage for life preservers, well marked if not readily visible, with child's life preservers separately stowed.
20. Provide an appropriate number of approved-type 24-inch ring buoys with water, light, and 60 feet of line.
21. Provide six red and six orange hand-held flares, or twelve hand-held combination flare and smoke distress signals of approved type and current date.

22. Provide a portable watertight container for flares.
23. Provide a hand-portable 5 GPM (minimum) fire pump.
24. Provide an installed CO_2 system for the machinery and fuel tank spaces if using gasoline.
25. Provide one B-1 extinguisher for wheelhouse, one B-1 extinguisher for gasoline machinery spaces, two B-2 extinguishers for diesel machinery spaces without installed CO_2 systems, one B-2 extinguisher for each accommodation and/or galley space, all to be of USCG- or UL- marine approved type.
26. Remount all electric motors, switches, wiring, and other potential spark-producers as high above the bilges as practicable.
27. Provide approved backfire traps and drip pans with flameproof screens under updraft carburetors and filters of all gasoline machinery.
28. Provide metal marine-type strainers for gasoline lines. Strainers shall be of the type opening on top for cleaning screens. A drip pan fitted with flame screen shall be installed under the strainer.
29. Provide suitable insulation and/or coolant for exhaust pipes.
30. Install suitable fuel tanks or provide data and prove existing tanks to be in reasonable compliance for fuel used and amount carried.
31. Provide $1\frac{1}{2}$ -inch diameter, electrically bonded fuel fill pipes, rigged to permit sounding of tanks and prevent an overflow of liquid or vapor from entering the inside of the vessel.
32. Provide vent lines for fuel tanks, to be of $\frac{3}{4}$-inch O.D. tube minimum for gasoline, and no less than $\frac{5}{8}$-inch O.D. tube for diesel tanks.
33. Provide marked emergency shutoff valves at fuel tanks, operable from the weather deck.
34. Provide fuel flex lines or loops at engines.
35. Permanently seal closed all means of drawing gasoline below deck; provide a plugged or capped valve at all diesel water traps or strainers to prevent fuel leakage.
36. Remove all petcocks from diesel and gasoline fuel systems. Provide metal-seating screw-down valves.
37. Provide 30-by-30-mesh-per-inch flameproof screens at fuel tank vents.
38. Prior to installation, fuel tanks vented to the atmosphere shall be tested to and withstand a pressure of 5 PSI or one and a half times the maximum head to which they may be subjected in service, whichever is greater.
39. Provide a bilge suction system, with separate lines, check valves, and strainers for each water-tight compartment. Operating valves are to be centrally grouped or manifolded and readily accessible.
40. Provide an accessible valve aft of collision bulkhead at bilge line penetration.
41. Provide a bilge pump in accordance with 46 CFR Table 182.25-10 (a).
42. Provide an emergency hand tiller for single-screw vessels.
43. Provide an interlocked ignition and vent-exhaust blower switch for each gasoline engine.
44. Provide lead- or plastic-lined battery boxes for batteries, at least 10-inch headroom, checked to prevent shifting of batteries, effectively screened or boxed if in same compartment with gasoline machinery, and well vented.

45. All connections shall be made to the battery terminals with permanent-type connections.
46. Provide National Electric Code-type accessories, such as fuses, switches, and sockets to be listed or equivalent to UL types.
47. Remove all dead and unused wire. All wiring smaller than #14 AWG shall be removed from the vessel.
48. Provide junction boxes for all wire splices not made in fixtures or switch panels.
49. Provide an electrical bonding or grounding system joining all major metal components of the vessel, including fuel tanks, lines, electrical motors, radio, ground-plate, engine, and rudder-stock.
50. The electrical system shall be either over 50 volts or under 50 volts.
51. Remove all liquefied petroleum fuel or gasoline heating and cooking fixtures from the vessel.
52. Provide navigation lights and shapes, whistles, foghorns, and fog bells as required by the applicable Rules of the Road.
53. Provide adequate ground tackle.
54. Provide a suitable compass.
55. Provide a radio telephone with current FCC station and personnel licenses.
56. Provide emergency lighting by fixed or portable battery lamps.
57. Post emergency instructions.
58. Post operator licenses and certificates of inspection under glass in a place accessible to passengers. Ensure that certification expiration-date stickers are properly posted.
59. Attach retroreflective material on life jackets, and provide lights if route is over 20 miles from a harbor of safe refuge.
60. Any vessel fitted with a toilet is required to have an approved marine sanitation device.
61. Have onboard vessel documentation with service of vessel showing passengers or certificate of numbers if vessel is under 5 net tons.
62. Provide emergency position-indicating radio beacon (EPIRB) for vessels in ocean and coastwise service.
63. Provide a fire ax if vessel is over 65 feet in length.
64. Provide adequate and up-to-date charts for areas of operation.
65. Adequately mark the hull, lifesaving gear, emergency escapes, and fuel shutoff valves.

APPENDIX E

Lending Terms

TYPES OF MONEY

Lenders usually categorize money as *trade credit*, *short-term money*, *long-term money*, or *equity capital*.

Trade credit is money owed suppliers who permit a charter operator to carry fast-moving inventory on open account. Fuel, provisions, ship's store's inventory, or fish bait might be carried on open account. A track record of good trade credit is proven evidence of ability to repay borrowed funds.

Short-term loans are used for purchases of inventory for special reasons, such as the upcoming season's inventory. Such loans are self-liquidating because they generate sales dollars and are repaid in less than a year. A short-term loan might be used for slow-moving ship's stores, or perhaps for a one-time publicity promotion designed to bring in charterers during a special community celebration.

Long-term borrowing—for more than a year—provides money for expansion or modernization. Long-term money is paid back in periodic installments from profits. A charter operator might buy a new boat through long-term credit.

Equity (investment) *capital* is money obtained by selling an interest in the business. You don't repay equity capital. Instead, you take people into the company who are willing to risk their money. They are interested in potential income, rather than an immediate return on their investment. Equity capital often comes from bringing in a partner or partners, or through stock sales (see also section later in this appendix on venture capital).

COLLATERAL

The unsecured loan is the most frequently used form of short-term bank credit. No collateral is used because the bank relies upon the charter operator's credit reputation. However, many short-term and long-term loans will require collateral. Such *secured loans* involve a signature of an endorser, comaker, or guarantor, or a pledge of assets or securities, or both.

Types of Collateral

An *endorser* is contingently liable for the note. If the borrower fails to pay, the bank expects the endorser to make the note good.

A *comaker* creates an obligation jointly with the borrower. The bank can collect directly from either the maker or the comaker.

A *guarantor* guarantees payment of a note by signing a guaranty commitment. Banks often require guarantees from officers of corporations in order to assure continuity of effective management. A guarantor for a yacht-charter operator might be the manufacturer of the operator's yacht or yachts.

An *assigned lease* is similar to a guarantee. In a charter operation, the lender provides the money for a vessel; then the buyer and seller negotiate a lease, which is assigned so that the lender receives the lease payments.

A *warehouse receipt* is normally used for merchandise that can be marketed readily. Such a receipt assures the bank that the collateral merchandise either has been placed in a public warehouse or has been left on the borrower's premises under the control of a bonded employee.

A *trust receipt* is security for a note used in floor planning. For example, a charter operator who decides to sell a certain line of boats might arrange with the manufacturer and a lender to place models in the showroom or at the docks. The operator signs a trust receipt in acknowledging receipt of the vessels, agrees to keep them in trust for the lender, and promises to pay the lender as they are sold.

A *chattel mortgage* can be used to secure personal property, which is almost any tangible property other than real estate.

A *real estate mortgage*—for property used in the business or other property owned by the charter operator—can be used as collateral for a long-term loan.

Accounts receivable, normally for goods sold, are accepted as collateral by some banks, as well as agents called *factors*.

Savings accounts and *credit union accounts* can be assigned to a lender for collateral. Depending upon the conditions of the loan, the borrower may continue to earn interest on the savings account, thus reducing the net cost of the loan.

A *life insurance policy* can be assigned to a bank as collateral, usually for a loan up to the cash value of the policy.

Stocks and *bonds* can be used as collateral if they are marketable. If the market value drops below the bank's required margin, it may ask for additional security or payment.

LOAN COVENANTS

If the lender evaluates your charter operation as a good risk, the ensuing loan may have a minimum of limitations as to repayment terms, pledging of security, or periodic reporting. However, if the risk appears to be a poor one, the lender will seek more limitations, which will be written into the loan agreement as *covenants*. Here are some negative covenants, or restrictions on actions by the borrower that require prior approval from the lender.

- No further additions to total debt.
- No pledging or further pledging of assets.
- No issuance of dividends in excess of terms specified in the loan agreement.

Positive covenants also place limitations on the borrower. They spell out things that the borrower must agree to do, such as:

- Maintain a minimum of net working capital.
- Carry a specified amount of insurance.
- Repay the loan according to terms in the agreement.
- Supply the lender with periodic financial statements and reports.

Terms can be negotiated, and limitations in a loan agreement can be amended later, but the loan agreement you sign is one with which you might have to operate for a long time.

Don't hesitate to question a restrictive clause, particularly if it is part of a preprinted form used for the loan agreement. It may be more important to your business to have it deleted than it is to the lender to keep it.

VENTURE CAPITAL

A charter operator seeking a large amount of front-end equity capital—generally $250,000 or more—might contact a *venture-capital* firm. Venture-capital firms deal only in projects of larger sizes because of the high cost of investigation and administration.

Venture capital is a risky business for the lender, because it is difficult to judge the worth of a company in its early stage. Therefore, most venture-capital firms set rigorous policies, often accepting for investment less than one percent of the proposals they receive. They invest for long-term capital growth; thus they become owners, holding stock or other securities in the company. They probably will insist on having a say in major business decisions and will likely lead the operator on the road to selling out eventually or going public.

APPENDIX F

Return on Promotion and Break-even Analysis

RETURN ON PROMOTION (ROP)

The simple case studies that follow were created to assist with calculating ROP and break-even formulas. The sample formulas used can be incorporated into a single computer spreadsheet for easy computation. ROPs derived allow for quick comparisons of multiple promotions, regardless of the differences in the variables of overall promotion cost, responses, and orders.

The formulas can also be used to bring differences in circulation and insertion costs among several publications into common ROPs, by applying the same estimated response and order rate to each.

Formulas

Formula 1. Cost Per Thousand Direct-mail Addressees

$$\text{CPM} = \frac{\text{total direct-mail cost}}{\text{number of pieces mailed}} \times 1{,}000$$

Formula 1A. Cost Per Thousand Readers, Television Viewers, or Radio Listeners

$$\text{CPM} = \frac{\text{ad preparation cost} + \text{insertion cost}}{\text{number of readers, viewers, or listeners}} \times 1{,}000$$

Formula 2. Responses Per Thousand Recipients

$$\text{RPM} = \frac{\text{total responses}}{\text{total recipients} / 1{,}000}$$

Formula 3. Orders Per Thousand Recipients

$$\text{OPM} = \frac{\text{total orders}}{\text{total recipients} / 1{,}000}$$

Formula 4. Cost Per Order

$$\text{CPO} = \frac{\text{CPM}}{\text{OPM}}$$

Formula 5. Percentage of Return on Promotion

$$\text{ROP} = \frac{\text{normal net profit per sale} - \text{cost per order} \times 1{,}000}{\text{cost per order}}$$

Case 1

Return on a Direct-mail Promotion. Captain Chartermore's profit-and-loss statement discloses that he currently earns a net profit of $20 for every $100 charter he sells. He completes a direct-mail distribution of eight hundred postcards. Postcards and printing cost 22 cents each, including postage. He receives a 3 percent response rate, or twenty-four responses, nineteen of which are redeeming the card with a charter order. What would Captain Chartermore's ROP tell us?

Formula 1: $\frac{800 \times .22}{800} \times 1{,}000 = \$220 \text{ (CPM)}$

Formula 2: $\frac{24}{800} \times 1{,}000 = 30 \text{ (RPM)}$

Formula 3: $\frac{19}{800} \times 1{,}000 = 23.75 \text{ (OPM)}$

Formula 4: $\frac{220}{23.75} = \$9.26 \text{ (CPO)}$

Formula 5: $\frac{20 - 9.26}{9.26} \times 100 = 116\% \text{ (ROP)}$

Case 2

Return on a Newspaper Ad. Captain Chartermore places an ad in a local paper with a circulation of two thousand five hundred. Insertion cost is $200 and the neighborhood printer charges $25 to prepare the ad. He receives seventy-five responses and twenty of those buy a charter. How does Captain Chartermore's ROP compare with Case 1?

Formula 1A: $\frac{25 + 200}{2{,}500} \times 1{,}000 = \$90 \text{ (CPM)}$

Formula 2: $\frac{75}{2{,}500} \times 1{,}000 = 30 \text{ (RPM)}$

Formula 3: $\frac{20}{2{,}500} \times 1{,}000 = 8 \text{ (OPM)}$

Formula 4: $\frac{90}{8} = \$11.25 \text{ (CPO)}$

Formula 5: $\frac{20 - 11.25}{11.25} \times 100 = 77\% \text{ (ROP)}$

BREAK-EVEN ANALYSIS

The break-even quantity is a reference point for judging the feasibility of a proposed direct-mail effort. It is the number of units with a known gross margin that must be sold in order to cover all fixed costs plus all direct-mail costs. It can be found using the following formula:

$$\text{Break-even quantity} = \frac{\text{total fixed costs} + \text{direct-mail costs}}{\text{unit gross margin}}$$

Fixed costs are costs that do not increase when units are sold and must be paid even if no units are sold. Break-even analysis determines the number of units that must be sold to cover fixed costs.

Direct-mail costs are variable costs that are attributed directly to each unit that is sold when the order is fulfilled. They include such items as costs of merchandise, handling, delivery, and taxes.

Unit gross margin is the remainder after subtracting direct-mail costs (variable costs) from the selling price.

Determining Number of Orders That Must Be Received in Order to Generate the Break-even Quantity

If historically 10 percent of orders are returned and 5 percent result in bad debt, then:

$$\text{Break-even orders} = \frac{\text{break-even quantity}}{(1-.10)\,(1-.05)}$$

$$\text{Break-even response rate} = \frac{\text{break-even orders}}{\text{number of mailings}}$$

If the response rate is likely to be achieved, the campaign should be considered further.

APPENDIX G

SBA Online—Small Business Administration's Online Service

As of January 1996, the SBA offered files for downloading and other information via the telephone numbers shown below. Additionally, the SBA offers full use of its online service to Internet users at sbaonline.sba.gov. The Internet service is at no charge from SBA.

The following categories of files are available for downloading via 800-697-4636:

1. Women
2. International Trade
3. Veterans
4. General Business Development Files
5. Business Initiatives, Education, and Training
6. Service Corps of Retired Executives (SCORE)
7. Government Contracting
8. Minority Small Business
9. Small Business Innovation Research
10. Surety Guarantee
11. Small Business Investment
12. Financial Assistance
13. Disaster Assistance
14. Legislation and Regulations
15. Small Business Development Center Files
16. Miscellaneous Files
17. White House Files
18. Talk to Your Government Files
19. List of All SBA Online Files

The following additional categories of files are available for downloading via 900-463-4636 and 202-401-9600. The 900-number charge is 14 cents for each minute, and the 202-number is at regular telephone company rates.

20. Files for Starting Up a Business
22. Files for Financing a Business
23. Files for Marketing Your Business
24. Files That Help Run Your Business
25. Miscellaneous File Uploads
26. New Files
27. List of All SBA Online Files
28. Access to SBA Online Information
29. Internet Information Files

APPENDIX H

Suspension and Revocation Guidelines for Administrative Law Judges

This table, published in Part 5 of 46 CFR, expresses the ranges (in months, if not revoked) considered appropriate for a particular act or offense prior to the judge's considering matters in mitigation or aggravation, or considering whether the respondent is a repeat offender.

*In cases of findings of incompetence or dangerous drug violations, the reference advises, "Revocation is the only proper order."

TYPE OF OFFENSE	RANGE
MISCONDUCT:	
Failure to obey master's/ship officer's order.	1–3
Failure to comply with U.S. law or regulations.	1–3
Possession of intoxicating liquor.	1–4
Failure to obey master's written instruction.	2–4
Improper performance of duties related to vessel safety.	2–5
Failure to join vessel (required crew member).	2–6
Violent acts against other persons (without injury).	2–6
Failure to perform duties related to vessel safety.	3–6
Theft.	3–6
Violent acts against other persons (injury).	4–Revocation
Use, possession, or sale of dangerous drugs.	* Revocation
NEGLIGENCE:	
Negligently performing duties related to vessel navigation.	2–6
Negligently performing nonnavigational duties related to vessel safety.	1–3
Neglect of vessel navigation duties.	3–6
Neglect of nonnavigational safety-related duties.	2–4
Incompetence.	Revocation
VIOLATION OF REGULATION:	
Refusal to provide specimens for required chemical test.	12–24
Dangerous drugs (46 U.S.C. 7704).	* Revocation

APPENDIX I

U.S. Coast Guard Addresses

Part I lists district offices. Part II contains a listing of the marine safety center in Washington, D.C.; marine inspection offices; marine safety offices; and marine safety detachments. Part III lists regional examination centers. With the exception of the district offices, which are in order by district, all are listed alphabetically by state.

I. COAST GUARD DISTRICT OFFICES

1st Coast Guard District
408 Atlantic Avenue
Boston, MA 02110

2nd Coast Guard District
1222 Spruce Street
St. Louis, MO 63103

5th Coast Guard District
431 Crawford Street
Portsmouth, VA 23704

7th Coast Guard District
909 S.E. 1st Avenue
Miami, FL 33131

8th Coast Guard District
501 Magazine Street
New Orleans, LA 70130

9th Coast Guard District
1240 East 9th Street
Cleveland, OH 44199

11th Coast Guard District
501 West Ocean Blvd.
Long Beach, CA 90822

13th Coast Guard District
913 2nd Avenue, Suite 3352
Seattle, WA 98174

14th Coast Guard District
300 Ala Moana Blvd.
Honolulu, HI 96850

17th Coast Guard District
P.O. Box 25517
Juneau, AK 99802

II. MARINE SAFETY CENTER, MARINE INSPECTION OFFICES, MARINE SAFETY OFFICES, AND MARINE SAFETY DETACHMENTS

STATE	CITY AND ZIP CODE		ADDRESS
	American Samoa	96799	USCG Marine Safety Detachment, P.O. Box 249, Pago Pago
AK	Kodiak	99619-5000	USCG Marine Safety Detachment, c/o CG Support Center, P.O. Box 5A
AK	Anchorage	99501-1946	USCG Marine Safety Office, 510 L Street, Suite 100
AK	Sitka	99835-7554	USCG Marine Safety Detachment, 329 Harbor Drive, Room 202, Lloyd Center
AK	Valdez	99686-0486	USCG Marine Safety Office, P.O. Box 486
AK	Juneau	99801-8545	USCG Marine Safety Office, 2760 Sherwood Lane, Suite 2A
AK	Ketchikan	99901	USCG Marine Safety Detachment, 2030 Sealevel Drive, Suite 203
AK	Kenai	99611-7716	USCG Marine Safety Detachment, 150 Trading Bay Road, Suite #3
AL	Mobile	36652-2924	USCG Marine Safety Office, Ryan Walsh Bldg., 2nd Floor, P.O. Box 2924
AP	FPO Guam	96540-1056	USCG Marine Safety Office, PSC 455, Box 176
CA	Concord	94520-5001	USCG Marine Safety Detachment, Bldg. 188, Naval Weapons Station, 10 Delta Street
CA	San Diego	92101-1064	USCG Marine Safety Office, 2710 Harbor Drive, North
CA	Alameda	94501-5100	USCG Marine Safety Office, Bldg. 14, Coast Guard Island
CA	Long Beach	90802-1096	USCG Marine Safety Office, 165 North Pico Avenue
CA	Santa Barbara	93109-2397	USCG Marine Safety Detachment, 111 Harbor Way
DC	Washington	20590-0001	USCG Marine Safety Center, 400 7th Street S.W.

STATE	CITY AND ZIP CODE		ADDRESS
FL	Jacksonville	32206-3497	USCG Marine Safety Office, Room 213, 2831 Talleyrand Avenue
FL	Miami	33130-1608	USCG Marine Safety Office, Claude Pepper Federal Bldg., 51 SW 1st Avenue, 5th Floor
FL	Tampa	33606-3598	USCG Marine Safety Office, 155 Columbia Drive
GA	Savannah	31412-8191	USCG Marine Safety Office, P.O. Box 8191
HI	Honolulu	96813-4909	USCG Marine Safety Office, 433 Ala Moana Blvd., Room 1
IA	Davenport	52801-1513	USCG Marine Safety Detachment, Federal Bldg., Room 332, 131 East 4th Street
IL	Burr Ridge	60521-7059	USCG Marine Safety Office, 215 West 83rd Street, Suite D
KY	Louisville	40202-2230	USCG Marine Safety Office, 600 Martin Luther King Jr. Place, Room 360
KY	Paducah	42003-0170	USCG Marine Safety Office, 225 Tully Street
LA	New Orleans	70112-2711	USCG Marine Safety Office, 1440 Canal Street
LA	Morgan City	70380-1304	USCG Marine Safety Office, 800 David Drive, Room 232
LA	Houma	70360-4805	USCG Marine Safety Office, 425 Lafayette Street, Room 204
LA	Baton Rouge	70801-1999	USCG Marine Safety Office, 626 Main Street
LA	Lake Charles	70601-5612	USCG Marine Safety Office, Port of Lake Charles, 150 Marine Street
MA	Boston	02109-1096	USCG Marine Safety Office, 447 Commercial Street
MD	Baltimore	21202-4022	USCG Marine Safety Office, Custom House
ME	Portland	04112-0108	USCG Marine Safety Office, P.O. Box 108
MI	Detroit	48207-4380	USCG Marine Safety Office, 110 Mt. Elliott Avenue

STATE	CITY AND ZIP CODE		ADDRESS
MI	Sault Ste. Marie	49783-9501	USCG Marine Safety Office, c/o CG Group
MN	Duluth	55802-2352	USCG Marine Safety Office, Canal Park
MN	St. Paul	55165-0428	USCG Marine Safety Office, P.O. Box 65428
MO	St. Louis	63103-2835	USCG Marine Safety Office, 1222 Spruce Street
MP	Saipan	96950-5000	USCG Marine Safety Detachment, Emergency Operations Center, Capitol Hill
MS	Greenville	38701-9586	USCG Marine Safety Detachment, 1801 Industrial Park Road
NC	Wilmington	28401-3907	USCG Marine Safety Office, Suite 500, 272 North Front Street
NY	Massena	13662-0728	USCG Marine Safety Detachment, Box 728, 180 Andrews Street
NY	Buffalo	14202-2395	USCG Marine Safety Office, Room 1111, Federal Bldg., 111 West Huron Street
NY	New York	10004-1466	USCG Marine Safety Office, Battery Park Building
OH	Cincinnati	45204-1094	USCG Marine Safety Detachment, 4335 River Road
OH	Cleveland	44114-1092	USCG Marine Safety Office, 1055 East Ninth Street
OH	Toledo	43604-1590	USCG Marine Safety Office, Federal Bldg., Room 101, 234 Summit Street
OR	Portland	97217-3992	USCG Marine Safety Office, 6767 North Basin Avenue
PA	Pittsburgh	15222-1371	USCG Marine Safety Office, Suite 700, Kossman Bldg., Forbes Avenue and Stanwix Street
PA	Philadelphia	19147-4395	USCG Marine Safety Office, 1 Washington Avenue
PR	Old San Juan	00902-3666	USCG Marine Safety Office, P.O. Box S-3666
RI	Providence	02903-1790	USCG Marine Safety Office, John O. Pastore Federal Bldg.

STATE	CITY AND ZIP CODE		ADDRESS
SC	Charleston	29401-1817	USCG Marine Safety Office, 196 Tradd Street
TN	Memphis	38103-2300	USCG Marine Safety Office, 300 Jefferson Avenue, Suite 1301
TN	Nashville	37228-1700	USCG Marine Safety Detachment, 220 Great Circle Road, Suite 148
TX	Houston	77017-6595	USCG Marine Inspection Office, 8876 Gulf Freeway, Suite 210
TX	Port Arthur	77640-2099	USCG Marine Safety Office, Federal Bldg., 2875 75th Street and Hwy. 69
TX	Galena Park	77547-0446	USCG Marine Safety Office, P.O. Box 446
TX	Corpus Christi	78403-1621	USCG Marine Safety Office, P.O. Box 1621
TX	Galveston	77550-1705	USCG Marine Safety Office, Room 301, Post Office Bldg., 601 Rosenberg
VA	Norfolk	23510-1888	USCG Marine Safety Office, Norfolk Federal Bldg., 200 Granby Mall
VI	St. Thomas	00801-0818	USCG Marine Safety Detachment, P.O. Box 818
WA	Seattle	98134-1192	USCG Marine Safety Office, 1519 Alaskan Way South, Bldg. 1
WI	Sturgeon Bay	54235-0446	USCG Marine Inspection Office, 57 North 12th Avenue, P.O. Box 446
WI	Milwaukee	53207-1997	USCG Marine Safety Office, 2420 South Lincoln Memorial Drive
WV	Huntington	25701-2420	USCG Marine Safety Office, 1415 6th Avenue

III. REGIONAL EXAM CENTERS

STATE	CITY AND ZIP CODE		ADDRESS
	Piti, Guam	96910	USCG Marine Safety Office (MU), 1026 Cabras Hwy., Suite 102
AK	Ketchikan	99901	Supervisor (MU), USCG Marine Safety Detachment, 2030 Sealevel Drive, Suite 203
AK	Anchorage	99501-1946	USCG Marine Safety Office (REC), 510 L Street, Suite 100

STATE	CITY AND ZIP CODE		ADDRESS
AK	Juneau	99801-8545	USCG Marine Safety Office (REC), 2760 Sherwood Lane, Suite 2A
CA	Alameda	94501-5100	USCG Marine Safety Office (REC), Bldg. 14, Room 109, Coast Guard Island
CA	Long Beach	90802-1096	USCG Marine Safety Office (REC), 165 North Pico Avenue
FL	Miami	33130-1609	USCG Marine Safety Office (REC), Claude Pepper Federal Bldg., 6th Floor 51 SW 1st Avenue
HI	Honolulu	96813-4909	USCG Marine Safety Office (REC), Room 1, 433 Ala Moana Blvd.
LA	New Orleans	70112-2711	USCG Marine Safety Office (REC), 1440 Canal Street, 8th Floor
MA	Boston	02109-1045	USCG Marine Safety Office (REC), 455 Commercial Street
MD	Baltimore	21202-4022	USCG Marine Safety Office (REC), U.S. Custom House, 40 South Gay Street
MO	St. Louis	63103-2835	USCG Marine Safety Office (REC), 1222 Spruce Street, Suite 1215
NY	New York	10004-1466	USCG Marine Safety Office (REC), Battery Park Bldg.
OH	Toledo	43604-1590	USCG Marine Safety Office (REC), Room 501, Federal Bldg., 234 Summit Street
OR	Portland	97217-3992	USCG Marine Safety Office (REC), 6767 North Basin Avenue
PR	Old San Juan	00902-3666	USCG Marine Safety Office (MU), P.O. Box S-3666
SC	Charleston	29401-1899	USCG Marine Safety Office (REC), 196 Tradd Street
TN	Memphis	38106-2300	USCG Marine Safety Office (REC), 200 Jefferson Avenue, Suite 1302
TX	Houston	77017-6541	USCG Marine Safety Office (REC), 8876 Gulf Freeway, Suite 200
VA	Norfolk	23510-1888	USCG Marine Safety Office (MU), Norfolk Federal Bldg., 200 Granby Mall
WA	Seattle	98134-1192	USCG Marine Safety Office (REC), 1519 Alaskan Way South, Bldg. 1

Notes

INTRODUCTION

1. Fred Edwards, *Charter Your Boat for Profit* (Centreville, Md.: Cornell Maritime Press), 1989.
2. Jeffrey C. Smith, Executive Director, National Association of Charterboat Operators, 655 15th Street, NW, Suite 310, Washington, D.C., (202) 546-6993.
3. Information compiled from *No Cost Boating*, by Rod Gibbons; and from Clyde and Bette Rice, Wharfside Bed & Breakfast, P.O. 1212, Friday Harbor, WA 98250, (206) 378-5661.
4. Information compiled from *No Cost Boating*, by Rod Gibbons; and from brochure package "Tugboat *M.V. Challenger*—Sleep on Water—Bunk and Breakfast." Contact Jerry Brown, *M.V. Challenger*, 1001 Fairview Avenue North, Seattle, WA 98109, (206) 340-1201.
5. In *No Cost Boating*, Brown reports that on his vessel each room must have two entrances per cabin and must be above deck.
6. Barefoot Cay Marina, 100 Morris Avenue, Key Largo, FL 33037, (305) 451-5400.
7. Information obtained by interview with Captain Dave Zalewski, captain of fishing vessel *Lucky Too*; and from news story, "He'll Take You Fishing or to Scatter Ashes," in *St. Petersburg Times*, March 15, 1994.
8. "Any Takers?" *WorkBoat Magazine*, September/October 1994.
9. "High Stakes on the High Seas," *St. Petersburg Times*, St. Petersburg, FL, July 2, 1995.
10. Nautor's Swan Charters, 55 America's Cup Avenue, Newport, Rhode Island 02840, (800) 356-7296. Nautor's brochure states that Nautor's is a wholly owned subsidiary of Oy Nautor Ab, the Finnish builders of Swan. The fleet is located in St. Martin, in the French Antilles, but boats can be delivered to various Caribbean ports.
11. Lynn Jachney, Lynn Jachney Yacht Charters, P.O. Box 302, Marblehead, MA 01945, (800) 223-2050.
12. Natalie and Bob Tate, Chicagoland Bareboaters Club, Ltd., 2614 Princeton Avenue, Evanston, IL 60201, (800) 767-8760.
13. BOAT/U.S. Yacht Charters, 880 South Pickett Street, Alexandria VA 22304, (800) 477-4427.
14. CYOA, 6136 Frydenhoj 76, Saga Haven Marina, St. Thomas, VI 00802-1402, (800) 944-2962.
15. Mike Kimball, CPA and Roger Smith, CPA, *Tax Guide for the Business Use of Yachts, Volume II: Charter Operations*, Tax Savvy Publications, Ltd., (903) 561-9555.
16. Tom Christensen, WhyCharter Boat Exchange, Ltd, 23232 Peralta #103, Laguna Hills, CA 92653, (800) WHY-CHARTER.

17. Mike McCrory owns The Dive Shop II, 1222 Westpark Drive, Little Rock, AR 72204, (800) 467-3483.
18. "Express Lanes," *WorkBoat Magazine*, November/December 1994.
19. Bill Miller, Miller's Marina, Campground, and Suwannee Houseboats, Suwannee, FL 32692, (800) 458-2628. Miller advised that waterborne visitors should enter the Suwannee by the well-marked McGriff channel within two hours of high tide, for a mean low water depth of 4 to 5 feet.
20. Captain Mike Bomar, Captain Mike's Watersports, P.O. Box 66214, St. Pete Beach, FL 33736, (813) 360-1998.
21. *The Kansas City Star*, September 4, 1994.
22. American Sailing Association, 13922 Marquesas Way, Marina del Rey, CA 90292, (310) 822-7171; and US SAILING, Box 209, Newport, RI 02840-0209, (800) 724-5011.

CHAPTER 1. STARTING YOUR BUSINESS

1. Peter Olsen, Counselor, SCORE Chapter 115, 800 31st Street North, St. Petersburg, FL 33701, (813) 327-7207.
2. A large part of this chapter was adapted from information contained in the Small Business Administration's (SBA) Publication MP-12, *Checklist for Going into Business*; and the SBA Online file OBDALL.TXT, *Business Start-up Considerations*, downloaded September 9, 1994. SBA Online can be reached by modem at (800) 697-4636, (900) 463-4636, or (202) 401-9600. The 900 number is 14 cents each minute, and the 202 number is at regular telephone company rates. SBA Online also can be reached on the Internet's World Wide Web at //www.sbaonline.sba.gov.
3. The six steps are an encapsulation of material in *Marketing Management* by Philip Kotler and *Bottom-Up Marketing* by Ries and Trout (*see* bibliography for full reference).
4. See chapter 6. Also see SBA publication MP-11, *Business Plan for Small Service Firms*; SBA publication MP-15, *The Business Plan for Home-based Business*; and one of the software packages, such as *Business Plan Master*, shareware software developed by David A. Works, (406) 862-1280.
5. IRS Publication 334: *Tax Guide For Small Businesses*, 1994, Ch. 29.
6. Ibid.
7. Ibid.
8. IRS Publication 542: *Tax Information on Corporations*, 1994.
9. SBA Publication MP-25: *Selecting the Legal Structure for Your Business.*
10. Extracted from "Becoming a Corporation May Make Sense for Your Firm," by Jeffrey C. Smith, *The NACO Report*, July/Aug. 1994.
11. SBA publication MP-12: *Checklist for Going into Business*, and SBA Online file OBDALL.TXT downloaded 9/94.
12. IRS Publication 583: *Taxpayers Starting a Business*, 1994.
13. Mike Kimball, CPA, Roger A. Smith, CPA, and Dr. Karen S. Lee, J.D., CPA, *Tax Guide for the Business Use of Yachts*. Kimball and Smith, *Volume II:*

Charter Operations, January 1995 ed. You can order the former at Outdoor Empire Publishing, Inc., (206) 624-3845; and the latter at Tax Savvy Publications, Ltd., (903) 561-9555.

14. Abstracted from *The NACO Report*, March/April 1994, and May/June 1994. At publication time the IRS was reviewing its common-law employee regulations with the intention of simplifying them.

CHAPTER 2. ACCOUNTING AND BUDGETING

1. Much of the remainder of this chapter extrapolates information contained in the following SBA business development publications: FM 3: *Basic Budgets for Profit Planning*; FM 4: *Understanding Cash Flow*; FM 6: *Accounting Services for Small Service Firms*; and FM 10: *Recordkeeping in Small Business.*
2. See current issue of IRS Pub 334: *Tax Guide for Small Businesses*, for full details of tax years and tax accounting methods.
3. To determine your liability, if any, see IRS Publication 505: *Tax Withholding and Estimated Tax*, and use IRS Form 1040-ES: *Estimated Tax for Individuals.*

CHAPTER 3. HOW TO PREPARE AN INSURANCE PLAN

1. Adapted from principles discussed in "Risk Management: Protecting Your Business," by Jennifer Daniels, *Wealth Builder Monthly*, October 1994.
2. Barry M. Snyder, P.A., Attorney at Law, 2020 NE 163rd Street, Suite 300, North Miami Beach, FL 33162. Snyder's booklet, "The Captain and the Law," is a major source for the information in this chapter on liability. The booklet is available to those who attend his classes on the subject.
3. See the Federal Maritime Lien Act, 46 U.S.C. 911-984, also known as the Ship Mortgage Act, 1920.
4. *Pierside Terminal Operators, Inc. v. M/V* Floridian, 389 F.Supp. 25 (E.D. Va. 1974).
5. The key actions involve saving maritime property (the vessel or her cargo) from "impending peril on the sea or recovering such property from actual loss, as in the case of shipwreck, from derelict, or recapture." *The Blackwall*, 77 U.S. 1 (1869).
6. 46 U.S.C. 971 (1920).
7. From "Old Hull, New Problems," by Paul McKelvey, *WorkBoat Magazine*, March/April 1995.
8. *McAllister v. Magnolia Petroleum Co.*, 357 U.S. 221, 78 S.Ct. 1201, 2 L.Ed.2d 1272 (1958).
9. Section 33 of the Merchant Marine Act of 1920, codified as 46 U.S.C. 688 (1920), with amendments.
10. 46 U.S.C. 688 (1920), with amendments. Also see Death on the High Seas Act, 46 U.S.C. 761-768 (1920).
11. *The Osceola*, 189 U.S. 158, 159, 23 S.Ct. 483, 47 L.Ed. 760 (1903); *Mahnich v. Southern Steamship Co.*, 321 U.S. 96, 64 S.Ct. 455, 88 L.Ed. 561 (1944); et al.

12. *Kermarec v. Transatlantique*, 358 U.S. 625, 79 S.Ct. 406,3 L.Ed.2d 550 (1959), et al.
13. *Moore v. American Scantic Line, Inc.*, 121F.2d 767 (2d Cir. 1941).
14. 49 U.S.C. 781, 782 (1950).
15. From *BOAT/U.S. Reports*, September 1994.
16. 49 CFR 172.700-704.
17. 29 CFR 1910.120.
18. MARPOL Treaty, Annex V, implemented by 33 CFR 151, 46 CFR 25, and 49 CFR 146.
19. The Federal Boat Safety Act of 1971 contains a model good samaritan clause for the states.
20. 46 U.S.C. 181.
21. Information for this section taken from "A Little Risky Business," by Tim Murphy, *Cruising World*, October 1994.
22. *The NACO Report*, January/February 1994.
23. Extracted from *The NACO Report*, March/April 1994.

CHAPTER 4. MARKETING TOOLS

1. This chapter draws upon the author's experience as a marketing manager, public relations consultant, and chairman of numerous executive-level committees. It was influenced by concepts contained in the following books and publications (full references are in the bibliography):

   Bottom-Up Marketing, by Al Ries and Jack Trout; *The Concept of Direct Marketing*, by Vin Jenkins; *The Copywriter's Handbook*, by Robert Bly; *Fundamentals of Direct Marketing*, by Edward J. McGee, et al.; *Guerrilla Marketing*, by Jay Conrad Levinson; *How to Advertise*, by Kenneth Roman and Jane Maas; *How to Write and Use Simple Press Releases That Work*, by Kathy Kelly; *Innovation & Entrepreneurship*, by Peter F. Drucker; *Marketing*, by Carl McDaniel, Jr; *Marketing Management, Analysis, Planning, Implementation & Control*, by Philip Kotler; *Marketing Planning and Strategy*, by Subhash C. Jain; *Marketing Planning Strategies: A Guide for the Small or Medium-Sized Company*, by C. Rice; *Marketing Strategy and Plans*, by David J. Luck and O. C. Ferrell; *Marketing Warfare*, by Al Ries and Jack Trout; *Marketing Without Advertising*, by Michael Phillips and Salli Rasberry; *Positioning: The Battle for Your Minds*, by Al Ries and Jack Trout; *Sell Copy*, by Webster Kuswa; and *Streetfighting; Low-Cost Advertising/Promotion Strategies for Your Small Business*, by Jeff Slutsky with Woody Woodruff.

CHAPTER 5. HOW TO WRITE A MARKETING PLAN

1. Information in this chapter was drawn primarily from the following sources:

   Business Plan Master, shareware software developed by David A. Works, (406) 862-1280; CompuServe 70400,153; America Online DAVIDW2959; Internet david_works@cup.portal.com.; Philip Kotler's *Marketing Management, Analysis, Planning, Implementation & Control*; SBA MP-11: *Business*

Plan for Small Service Firms; SBA MP-15: *Business Plan for Home-Based Businesses*; and the author's experience in preparing and using marketing plans as chairman of the marketing committee for a maritime training company with a gross margin in the seven digits.

CHAPTER 6. HOW TO WRITE A BUSINESS PLAN

1. Peter Olsen, Counselor, SCORE Chapter 115, 800 31st Street North, St. Petersburg, FL 33701 (813) 327-7207.
2. Mike McCrory, The Dive Shop II, 1222 Westpark Drive, Little Rock, AR 72204 (800) 467-3483.
3. The business plan outline and explanation was created primarily from information contained in the following sources: *Business Plan Master*, shareware software developed by David A. Works, (406) 862-1280; CompuServe 70400,153; America Online DAVIDW2959; Internet david_works@cup.portal.com.; Philip Kotler's *Marketing Management, Analysis, Planning, Implementation & Control*; SBA MP-11: *Business Plan for Small Service Firms*; SBA MP-15: *The Business Plan for Home-Based Businesses*; and the author's experience in preparing and using strategic plans and business plans as chairman of the executive committee and the marketing committee at a maritime training company with a gross margin in the seven digits.
4. Captain Memo's Pirate Cruise, Inc., Clearwater Marina, Clearwater Beach, FL 34630, (813) 446-2587.

CHAPTER 7. COMPUTER ASSISTANCE

1. Russ Walter, *The Secret Guide to Computers*, (617) 666-2666.
2. The remainder of this chapter draws upon information contained in SBA Online file *CYB.TXT*, downloaded 9/9/94; the principles used in *Business Plan Master*, shareware software developed by David A. Works, (406) 862-1280, CompuServe 70400,153, America Online DAVIDW2959, Internet david_works@cup.portal.com; and *How to Computerize Your Small Business With the Help of Office Depot*, published by PC Today/Peed Corporation, August 1994.
3. *How to Computerize Your Small Business With the Help of Office Depot*, published by PC Today/Peed Corporation, August 1994.

CHAPTER 8. BOAT REGISTRATION AND DOCUMENTATION

1. This chapter relies on 46 CFR Subchapter G: *Documentation and Measurement of Vessels*. Subchapter G is found in 46 CFR Parts 41-69.
2. U.S. Coast Guard COMDTPUB P16754.7: *Boating Statistics 1993* (September, 1994).
3. The Exclusive Economic Zone was established by Presidential Proclamation Numbered 5030, dated March 10, 1983 (48 FR 10105, 3 CFR, 1983).
4. For exceptions and grandfathering, see 46 CFR 67.21 (d) and 46 CFR 67.45.

5. The note following 46 CFR 67.23 says, "A vessel having a Certificate of Documentation endorsed only for recreation may be bareboat chartered only for recreational use. Guidance on the elements of a valid bareboat charter should be obtained through private legal counsel." The Passenger Vessel Safety Act of 1993 states that a recreational vessel may be chartered with no crew provided or specified by the owner so long as it carries no more than twelve passengers. See chapter 9 for further information.
6. Specifics of 883-1 citizenship for purposes of limited coastwise documentation endorsements are spelled out in 46 CFR Part 68: Documentation of Vessels Pursuant to Extraordinary Legislative Grants.
7. 46 CFR 67.167
8. 46 CFR Part 69.
9. From *BOAT/U.S. Reports*, July 1995.
10. 46 CFR 67.7.
11. Summarized from 33 CFR 2.05-25.

CHAPTER 9. BAREBOAT OR CREWED?

1. Information for this chapter was obtained from the *Passenger Vessel Safety Act of 1993* (PSVA of 1993) (codified in 46 U.S.C.), from Coast Guard Navigation and Vessel Inspection Circular (NVIC) No. 7-94, "Guidance on the Passenger Vessel Safety Act of 1993," and from 46 U.S.C., Section 2101.
2. PSVA of 1993, Section 502.
3. PSVA of 1993, Section 506.
4. PSVA of 1993, Section 507.

CHAPTER 10. INSPECTION AND CERTIFICATION

1. Information for this chapter was obtained from the *Passenger Vessel Safety Act of 1993* (codified in 46 U.S.C.); from 46 CFR, Subchapter A: *Procedures Applicable to the Public*; Subchapter B: *Merchant Marine Officers and Seamen*; Subchapter C: *Uninspected Vessels; Subchapter H: Passenger Vessels*; Subchapter K: *Small Passenger Vessels (Under 100 Gross Tons), 151 or more Passengers, Under 200 Feet in Length*; Subchapter S: *Subdivision and Stability*; Subchapter T: *Small Passenger Vessels (Under 100 Gross Tons)*; and from an article, "Special K," by Christine Rohn Hilston, *WorkBoat Magazine*, May/June 1994.
2. Captain Mike Bomar, Captain Mike's Watersports, P.O. Box 66214, St. Pete Beach, FL 33736, (813) 360-1998.

CHAPTER 11. CAPTAINS' LICENSES, CERTIFICATES, AND ENDORSEMENTS

1. Inspected vessel requirements: 46 CFR 15.103 (c); Types of vessels requiring inspection: 46 CFR 24.05-1 (a); Assistance towing vessels: 46 CFR 15.410;

Uninspected vessels carrying passengers for hire: 46 CFR 24.05–1 (a); Passengers for hire: 46 CFR 24.10-3; Passengers: 46 CFR 24.20-23; Navigable waters: 33 CFR 2.05-25. Navigable waters generally are any waters that have been used for commerce, that might be used for commerce, or that create a connection between two other bodies of navigable water. This means that, unless exempted, almost any inland water that will float a boat is navigable.

2. 46 U.S.C., Section 2101 (5a).
3. See 46 CFR Part 10, and *U.S. Coast Guard Licenses and Certificates*, by Gregory D. Szczurek.
4. 46 CFR 10.103.
5. The references are 46 CFR 10.429 and 46 CFR 10.456 for limited masters; 46 CFR 10.466 for limited six-packs.
6. Information about advanced licenses was not included in order to focus on the licenses needed by most charter captains. See 46 CFR Part 10 for more details. A comprehensive reference on the entire Coast Guard licensing system is *U.S. Coast Guard Licenses and Certificates* by Gregory D. Szczurek.

CHAPTER 12. OTHER REQUIREMENTS FOR BOATS AND CREWS

1. Vessel Bridge-to-Bridge Radiotelephone Act, 33 U.S.C. 1201-1208.
2. Information about FCC licensing requirements was abstracted from FCC Fact Sheet PR-5000, Federal Communications Commission, 1919 M Street, N.W., Washington, D.C. 20554.
3. 46 CFR 16.105.
4. 46 CFR 25 contains detailed requirements for personal flotation devices.
5. 46 CFR 25 contains detailed requirements for hand-portable fire extinguishers.
6. See 46 CFR 25 for additional requirements for fire-extinguishing systems in engine spaces.
7. Information obtained from U.S. Coast Guard Seventh District *Special Notice to Mariners (1994-1995).*
8. Ibid.
9. Excerpted and summarized from an article by the author for American Professional Captains Association, July 1986, P.O. Box 350398, Fort Lauderdale, FL 33316. The dive-boat skipper's name is omitted to avoid unnecessary embarrassment in a case that is now closed, but is a matter of record in U.S. Coast Guard Docket No. 07-0016-MEH-85, Case No. 16722.06.

CHAPTER 13. COAST GUARD INVESTIGATIONS AND HEARINGS

1. This chapter draws upon information contained in 46 CFR Part 4, *Marine Casualties and Investigations*; and Part 5, *Marine Investigation Regulations—Personnel Action.*
2. 46 CFR 4.07-5 requires "persons having knowledge of the subject matter of the investigation to answer questionnaires" and to produce "relevant books, papers,

documents and other records." Failure to do so may result in a charge of misconduct against the license holder.

3. 46 CFR 5.105.
4. 46 CFR 5.23; see 46 CFR 5.27, 5.29, 5.31, 5.33, and 5.57, respectively.
5. Information concerning administrative law judges was derived from 46 CFR 5.19.
6. Information for sections on prehearing, hearing, reopening, and appeals is found in 46 CFR Part 5, Subparts H, I, and J, respectively.
7. 46 CFR 5.59.
8. 46 CFR 5.61.
9. 46 CFR 5.9.

APPENDIX A. SELECTING A MARINE SURVEYOR

1. Information abstracted from *Seaworthy*, January 1995, BOAT/U.S.
2. Taken from brochures provided by The National Association of Marine Surveyors, Inc., P.O. Box 9306, Chesapeake, VA 23321-9306, (800) 822-NAMS; and The Society of Accredited Marine Surveyors, 4163 Oxford Avenue, Jacksonville, FL 32210, (800) 344-9077.

Bibliography

Bly, Robert W. *The Copywriter's Handbook.* New York: Henry Holt and Company, 1990.

Code of Federal Regulations (Titles 33 and 46). Washington, D.C.: GPO.

Communications Briefings. Pitman, N.J.: Communications Publications and Resources.

Drucker, Peter F. *Innovation & Entrepreneurship.* New York: Harper & Row, 1985.

Gibbons, Rod. *No Cost Boating.* Lake Oswego, Ore.: Island Educational Publishing, 1991.

Jain, Subhash C. *Marketing Planning and Strategy.* Cincinnati, Ohio: South-Western Publishing Company, 1985.

Jenkins, Vin. *The Concept of Direct Marketing.* Melbourne, Australia: Australia Post, 1984.

Kelly, Kathy. *How to Write and Use Simple Press Releases That Work.* New York: Visibility Enterprise, 1991.

Kimball, Mike, Roger A. Smith, and Karen S. Lee. *Tax Guide for the Business Use of Yachts.* Seattle, Wash.: Outdoor Empire Publishing, Inc., 1992

Kimball, Mike, and Roger A. Smith. *Tax Guide for the Business Use of Yachts, Volume II: Charter Operations.* Tyler, Tex.: Tax Savvy Publications, Ltd., 1994.

Kotler, Philip. *Marketing Management, Analysis, Planning, Implementation & Control.* Englewood Cliffs, N.J.: Prentice Hall, Inc., 1991.

Kuswa, Webster. *Sell Copy.* Cincinnati, Ohio: Writer's Digest Books, 1979.

Levinson, Jay Conrad. *Guerrilla Marketing.* New York: Houghton Mifflin Co., 1984.

Luck, David J., and O. C. Ferrell. *Marketing Strategy and Plans.* Englewood Cliffs, N.J.: Prentice-Hall, Inc., 1985.

McDaniel, Carl Jr. *Marketing.* 2d ed. San Francisco: Harper & Row, 1982.

McGee, Edward J., et al. *Fundamentals of Direct Marketing.* Englewood Cliffs, N.J.: Prentice Hall, Inc., 1967.

Phillips, Michael, and Salli Rasberry. *Marketing Without Advertising.* Berkeley, Calif.: Nolo Press, 1991.

Rice, C. *Marketing Planning Strategies: A Guide for the Small or Medium-Sized Company.* New York: Dartnell Corporation, 1984.

Ries, Al, and Jack Trout. *Bottom-Up Marketing.* New York: McGraw-Hill, Inc., 1989.

———. *Marketing Warfare.* New York: McGraw-Hill, 1986.

———. *Positioning: The Battle for Your Minds.* New York: McGraw Hill, 1986.

Roman, Kenneth, and Jane Maas. *How to Advertise.* New York: St. Martins Press, 1976.

Schwab, Victor O. *How to Write a Good Advertisement.* Los Angeles, Calif.: National Mail Order Association, 1991.

Slutsky, Jeff, with Woody Woodruff. *Streetfighting; Low-Cost Advertising/Promotion Strategies for Your Small Business.* Englewood Cliffs, N.J., Prentice-Hall, 1984.

Small Business Administration. *Accounting Services for Small Service Firms.* FM 6; *Basic Budgets for Profit Planning.* FM 4; *Business Plan for Home-based Business.* MP-15; *Business Plan for Small Service Firms.* MP-11; *Checklist for Going into Business.* MP-12; *Recordkeeping in Small Business.* FM 10; *Understanding Cash Flow.* FM 4.

Szczurek, Gregory D. *U.S. Coast Guard Licenses and Certificates.* New Orleans, La.: Azure Communications, 1988.

Walter, Russ. *The Secret Guide to Computers.* Somerville, Mass.: Russ Walter, 1991.

Index